How to Index Your
Local Newspaper Using
WordPerfect® or
Microsoft® Word for Windows®

How to Index Your Local Newspaper Using WordPerfect® or Microsoft® Word for Windows®

CARLA D. MORRIS
and
STEVEN R. MORRIS

1995
LIBRARIES UNLIMITED, INC.
Englewood, Colorado

This book is dedicated to the non-newsmaker who makes the local news and is never heard from again . . . at least not without a newspaper index!

LIBRARIES UNLIMITED, INC.
P.O. Box 6633
Englewood, CO 80155-6633
1-800-237-6124

Production Editor: Tama J. Serfoss
Copy Editor: Deborah W. Korte
Indexer: Christine J. Smith
Layout and Interior Design: Kay Minnis

Library of Congress Cataloging-in-Publication Data

Morris, Carla D.
    How to index your local newspaper using WordPerfect® or Microsoft®
Word for Windows® / by Carla D. Morris and Steven R. Morris.
    xvii, 167 p. 17x25 cm.
    ISBN 1-56308-305-1
    1. Newspapers--Abstracting and indexing--Computer programs.
2. Word processing. 3. WordPerfect (Computer file) 4. WordPerfect
for Windows (Computer file) 5. Microsoft Word. 6. Microsoft Word
for Windows. I. Morris, Steven R. II. Title.
Z695.655.M67   1995
025.4'907'0285436--dc20   95-21810
                                                                        CIP

Contents

DISK CONTENTS

Microsoft® Word 2.0 for Windows—filename: msw20win.doc

Preparing to Index
Formatting and Entering the Data
Preparing the Header
Beginning to Index
Sorting the Index into Alphanumeric Order
Printing the Index
Sample Index—filename: msw2wsmp.doc

Microsoft® Word 6.0 for Windows®—filename: msw60win.doc

Preparing to Index
Formatting and Entering the Data
Preparing the Header
Beginning to Index
Sorting the Index into Alphanumeric Order
Printing the Index
Sample Index—filename: msw6wsmp.doc

WordPerfect 6.0 for Windows—filename: wp60win.doc

Preparing to Index
Formatting and Entering the Data
Preparing the Header
Beginning to Index
Sorting the Index into Alphanumeric Order
Correcting Sorting Problems
Printing the Index
Macro Inventory
Sample Index—filename: wp60wsmp.doc

WordPerfect 6.1 for Windows—filename: wp61win.doc

Preparing to Index
Formatting and Entering the Data
Preparing the Header
Beginning to Index
Sorting the Index into Alphanumeric Order
Correcting Sorting Problems
Printing the Index
Macro Inventory
Sample Index—filename: wp61wsmp.doc

Foreword

I have spent many years grappling with newspaper indexing issues in the state of Utah. I have served on steering committees, written guidelines, and counseled libraries on how to index local newspapers. As consultant to the Utah State Library and the Utah State Library Association, I created an index that covers the major newspapers in the state. My indexing experience includes indexing my own city's newspaper, *The Herald Journal.*

I firmly believe in the value of indexing newspapers. Every community has a cache of information locked in the local library's newspaper microfilm drawer. But this information is of little value if one cannot access selected subject matter.

Thanks to Carla and Steve Morris's book, any library with either Microsoft® Word for Windows® or WordPerfect® for Windows or DOS software will be able to index the local newspaper. In turn, the local index will hold the key to unlocking recent and past community history to all who seek it.

Certainly, sophisticated indexing programs are available if monies can be found. Unfortunately, many of these software programs have disappeared, and the future of such programs is uncertain. For these reasons, the Morrises have chosen to use relatively inexpensive Microsoft and WordPerfect software for their indexing program. These programs—with some updates and upgrades—are likely to be around for some time.

This valuable book will enable you to turn your word-processing software into a valuable indexing instrument. Thanks to this work, any library or historical society can index in a cost-effective manner. I heartily recommend it!

—Warren Babcock, Reference Librarian
Utah State University, Merrill Library
(1993 Utah Librarian of the Year)

Preface

Having served as the reference librarian for the Provo City Library for 11 years, I have experienced great frustration—and a sense of embarrassment—when people ask me to produce facts, historical pictures, obituaries, and biographies pertinent to the city that the library serves. Only two basic histories of Provo exist, and historical photos had already been donated to Brigham Young University Special Collections. Therefore, the public library had little to offer in terms of local history.

I also felt sorry for young mothers who would come to the library, infant in tow, to search newspaper microfilm for birth announcements. After spending hours trying to find a particular birth announcement, many mothers left disappointed.

In 1980, librarian Helen Eastmond, her husband Dr. John Eastman, and I devised an Apple computer program to index *The Daily Herald,* using the most basic Sears subject headings. A few years later, the Provo Library agreed to participate in a pilot newspaper project spearheaded by the Utah State Library. Our task was to compile information (including date, headline, section, page, and column where the item could be found) from the daily newspaper and then save it on disk. Each month, the disks were sent to the Utah State Library, where they were sorted into alphanumerical order on a large mainframe computer. It sometimes took two to three months for the final product—a monthly hard copy of the index—to arrive back at the library. Surely there was an easier way to produce a monthly index in a timely manner.

Thus we began to explore simplifying the process so that we could not only input indexing information on a personal computer, but also process and print out the final product on the same computer. Simplifying the process meant minimizing the repetitive number of keystrokes encountered in indexing. My husband, Steve Morris, found a way to use WordPerfect 5.1 and customized macros to accomplish this.

Once our index of *The Daily Herald* was placed in the Provo City Library, interest in the concept of indexing local newspapers mushroomed in the library community. We received calls from other libraries in smaller cities interested in indexing their newspapers. It became increasingly clear that a manual explaining the concept and providing specifics on how to format and use a library's word-processing software to produce an index was needed. The result is this book, which provides a resource tool for those interested in indexing newspapers in a cost-effective manner by using a personal computer and existing software.

So I would like to welcome you to the challenge—and fun—of newspaper indexing. Over the years indexing has become an advocation for me more than a vocation. I consider indexing my hobby. I like indexing for the same reason I enjoy cross-stitching: The beauty of the work is realized in the attention to detail.

But indexing offers more gratifying and permanent results than cross-stitching could ever offer. The work you will do in indexing your local newspaper will enable legions of patrons, historians, family researchers, and countless others to explore and understand the history (and current events) of your community.

—Carla Morris

Acknowledgments

We wish to thank the past directors of Provo City Library, Larry Hortin and Howard Downey, who paid Carla's salary to create the index and make it available to the patrons of Provo City Library. We also wish to thank Lloyd Olsen of the Utah State Library, who had visions of a statewide index for Utah. His expertise and experience of a similar project completed in the state of Nevada proved very valuable. Warren Babcock provided inspiration and persistent nudging to produce this sourcebook for other librarians. Special thanks to Yvonne Stroup at the University of Utah Marriott Library, who graciously gave us permission to adapt her Subject Authority List for this publication. The articles, letters, and other material used as examples throughout the book were provided by *The Daily Herald* (Provo, Utah) and are reprinted by permission.

We also greatly appreciate the technical assistance we received in writing this book. We had to become familiar with other formats of WordPerfect and Microsoft Word, then write specific index formatting instructions for each program. A thank you to Novell's Earle Wells and to Steve Haenel of Libraries Unlimited for their help in applying the indexing process to Microsoft Word for Windows. Thanks also to Joy T. Horton and Richard W. Horton of Vernal, Utah, for their thoughts on microfilm indexing techniques.

Introduction

WHY INDEX THE NEWSPAPER?

Information relevant at the national, regional, or state level may be readily accessed in several databases and reference books. There is another category of information, however, that is far more elusive—local-interest items found in local newspapers. In the public's mind, there is no more reliable reference than the daily newspaper. The newspaper provides a consistent perspective of a community's history as it unfolds, encompassing the local news, letters to the editor, birth announcements, obituaries, sports, anniversaries, and other features. In many cases, it is often the only source of this kind of information.

This manual will include directions on indexing local newspapers, but the instructions can also be applied to indexing local magazines, historical reports, newsletters, court reports, police reports, or other local sources of information previously not indexed and therefore inaccessible. Using this manual, you will be able to create a valuable resource for the local library and the community it serves. Your indexing work will become a companion to the library's newspaper microfilm files. More importantly, the index, when used with the microfilm collection, will create an effective bridge of information that spans the past, present, and future.

HOW TO USE THIS BOOK

This manual is designed to provide both general information about how to index a local newspaper and specific information about using various versions of WordPerfect and Microsoft Word to create indexes. This manual, which will cover the guidelines behind indexing, is accompanied by a disk that contains files providing specific instructions in the formats of the word-processing program described. The word-processing programs discussed include WordPerfect 5.0

and 5.1 for DOS, WordPerfect 6.0 for Windows, WordPerfect 6.1 for Windows, Microsoft Word 2.0 for Windows, and Microsoft Word 6.0 for Windows. These files are designed to be printed out by the user (who will print only the applicable files) to provide detailed information on creating macros and preparing the program and the files for indexing.

Before you can begin indexing your local newspaper, you must first decide on the scope of your index, which describes what you *will* include and what you *will not* include. Chapter 1, "The Scope of the Local Newspaper Index," provides some guidelines and ideas for creating this scope. To further aid you, a sample scope with comments is included for your reference.

The next chapter, "Subject Headings," provides information on Library of Congress headings and shows you how to use appropriate Library of Congress subject headings in your index. Using sample articles, it explains how to determine which subject headings to use in an article that may have several. This chapter also discusses index style guidelines and details the rules and methods for indexing your newspaper. You will learn why you should use all capital letters in an index and how periods and dashes are used to organize the index headings and subheadings, including government and school subject headings and their respective departments. Finally, chapter 2 explains the techniques for entering editorial and photographic references.

Just like anything else, practice makes perfect. Indexing is no exception. Chapter 3, "Techniques for Indexing," offers some important instruction on how to perfect your skills as an indexer. This chapter addresses why consistency is the most important attribute of your index and how to achieve it. You will learn how to consistently refer to the major newsmakers in your index; how to effectively index from microfilm; how to deal with complex subject matter; and how to solve "quirky" problems of indexing, such as similar names in the same article, and so on.

The next chapter, "Indexing Samples That Illustrate How to Handle Various Situations," includes reprints of actual news stories—wedding and anniversary announcements, letters to the editor, editorials, obituaries, and reviews—and how they should be indexed. It also addresses some tricky situations: What do you do if the headline poorly describes the article? How do you index advertisements with a picture of the owner? It sometimes takes a little ingenuity to make the index useful and "patron friendly"!

Once you understand the concept of indexing, you will be ready to prepare your word-processing program to help some of the more repetitive parts of indexing easier—and faster. Chapter 5, "Preparing to Index Using Word-Processing Software," will help you format your document and set up macros for the indexing task. There's even a shortcut to get you started sooner, if you are familiar with your software page formatting applications.

The rest of chapter 5 is on disk, and for good reason: You are interested only in your version of WordPerfect or Microsoft Word, so why bother with any other formatting description? To finish this chapter, simply insert the disk in your computer and open the file that matches your word-processing software. Print that file out and keep it with this manual. The disk also contains a sample index in the format of your word-processing software, which you can use to prepare macros, or memorized keystrokes. At the conclusion of this chapter, both you and your computer should be ready to index.

Finally, indexing costs money. Some libraries are able to find funding for indexing projects; perhaps yours is, too. However, if you need to generate new money for a newspaper index, appendix A, "Getting Funding for Your Indexing Proposal," has some good ideas for planning and presenting a funding proposal. A sample proposal is included for your reference and to use as a template.

Appendix B is the Subject Authority File. This is an abbreviated list of subject headings to get you started. It has been provided in the manual for quick reference, with plenty of space for additions and insertions, and it is also found on your computer disk in both Microsoft Word and WordPerfect formats so that you can open the file onscreen while you do your indexing in another document. With Windows or a split-screen in DOS, you can have this file open for easy reference. As you decide on subject headings specific to your local issues, you can simply add these subject heading to the file, thus keeping it updated for your reference and making it meet your specific indexing needs.

Newspaper indexing is important work and extremely valuable for patrons, researchers, and historians. Don't put off creating the most valuable reference work in your library. Boot up your word-processing software and get started today!

1

The Scope of the Local Newspaper Index

Perhaps the most important and time-consuming part of indexing is determining the extent of the indexing project, which in turn dictates how much staff time can be allotted to the project. The parameters for the index—its scope—should be agreed upon by everyone involved in the indexing project. Decide specifically what will and will not be indexed and draft a proposal.

In defining the scope, it is sometimes useful to compare your scope proposal to a scope that has been tested and refined over a period of time. Warren Babcock of Utah State University has developed a scope style in his *Herald Journal Scope Manual.* This style is reflected in the following example of a scope document used to index *The Daily Herald* of Provo, Utah.

SCOPE FOR *THE DAILY HERALD* INDEX

Articles may be found under broad subject headings. Personal names or names of businesses or government bodies are used as subject headings. Articles are indexed under one of three areas, according to where the story occurred: Provo, Utah County, or Utah. Births are recorded under subject heading: BIRTHS—[NAME OF HOSPITAL WHERE BIRTH TOOK PLACE]. (Provo, Utah, has among the highest births per capita in the nation. The indexer may want to index under the name of the father or mother.)

This index includes actions, opinions, conditions, and photos of the people, places, and things making news in Utah County, as well as happenings reported in Wasatch, Juab, Summit, Sanpete, and Millard counties. Also included is a name index of obituaries, birth announcements, engagement announcements, wedding announcements, golden wedding anniversaries, and senior citizen birthday celebrations. These items will be of value to those interested in the history and culture of this area.

Topics to Be Indexed and Guidelines

Subject headings and subdivisions used in this index are taken from the *Library of Congress Subject Headings,* 13th edition. Personal names, names of businesses, government bodies, titles of plays, names of organizations, events titles, and geographical names are also used as subject headings.

Anniversaries: Indexed under the names of both the man and the woman. Indicate if accompanied by photo.

Business: Indexed under both the name of the business and the name of the individuals reported.

Court Reports: Indexed under COURTS as well as the personal names of offenders, judges, and attorneys that are reported. The headline/summary will include the offense, if it is reported.

Eagle Scouts: Indexed under the name of the scout. Indicate if accompanied by photo. Also listed under BOY SCOUTS—EAGLE SCOUT AWARDS.

Editorials: Indexed under the editor's name. Many editorials will be assigned a subject heading if the subject matter is included in the scope.

Engagements and Marriages: Indexed under name of the man and the woman. Indicate if accompanied by photo.

Government Bodies: Units beginning with phrases formed by generic terms plus the prepositions *of, on,* or *for* will be inverted: e.g., UTAH. WILDLIFE RESOURCES, DEPT. OF. Government departments, divisions, and boards are listed under the name of the appropriate government: e.g., PROVO. WOMEN'S COUNCIL OF. Government bodies with titles containing no prepositions will be indexed under the complete name: e.g., UTAH COUNTY PLANNING COMMISSION. One exception to all of the above is the heading PROVO OREM CHAMBER OF COMMERCE.

Honor Rolls. Indexed under the name of the school: e.g., DIXON MIDDLE SCHOOL—HONOR ROLL.

Military Personnel: Indexed under the last name of the person reported. Headline/summary will be MILITARY SERVICE.

Photographs: All local photographs will be indexed under the name of all persons identified in the photograph. The word PHOTO will appear at the end of the headline/summary statement.

Police Reports: Reports will be assigned a subject with the subdivision of the city where the incident took place: e.g., BURGLARY—PROVO; RAPE—OREM; or SHOOTING—AMERICAN FORK. In the case of theft, those items stolen will be listed in the headline when space allows. All police reports will be indexed by personal names of those involved, if the names are reported.

Reviews: Indexed under the name of the reviewer as well as the title of the work. Only local films, local plays, or books written by local authors will be indexed. If the work is reviewed by a local reviewer, the entire article will be indexed under the reviewer's name. The regular book review column by Howard Downey, the director of the Provo Library, will be listed under DOWNEY, HOWARD and PROVO. LIBRARY. The headline statement will be preceded by BOOK REVIEW: to avoid confusion with other news articles about the Provo City Library.

Schools: All school districts are indexed under name of district: e.g., PROVO SCHOOL DISTRICT. Articles dealing with specific schools will be indexed under the name of the school.

Sports: Indexed by name of school, with subdivision indicating the type of sport: e.g., BYU—FOOTBALL or PROVO HIGH SCHOOL—BASKETBALL.

Theatre: Indexed by THEATRE—[NAME OF CITY WHERE PLAY IS PERFORMED]: e.g., THEATRE—PROVO. If the play is performed by a school, it will be indexed under [NAME OF SCHOOL]—DRAMA. All plays are indexed under the title of the play.

Traffic Accidents: Indexed under TRAFFIC ACCIDENTS—[NAME OF CITY WHERE ACCIDENT OCCURRED]: e.g., TRAFFIC ACCIDENTS—PROVO. In addition, personal names will be indexed, if they are reported, and photos will be noted.

Topics Not to Be Indexed

Advertisements: Unless there is a related photo or article that would be considered historically significant.

Classified Ads: Unless a photo of a named person from the community is included.

Club Announcements: Unless historically significant activities, new officers, or prominent new members are listed. Specific people should be listed under both the club name and the personal name.

Foreign News: Unless there is a local connection to the story.

Legal Notices

National News: This can be obtained through *Facts on File*.

Pet of the Week

Recipes: Unless story features the cook or demonstrator or is accompanied by a photo of citizen or contest award winner.

Upcoming Events: These will be indexed when they occur.

Weather: Unless article summarizes the year's weather, unusual weather, or overall extreme conditions (for example, drought or floods).

COMMENTS ON THE SAMPLE SCOPE

Part of defining a scope is deciding to what extent each article should be indexed. The more entries per article, the longer the staff time spent on it, and the more expensive the project. Keep in mind who will be using the index; this will help you decide what should be indexed and in what order of priority.

You may choose to make parts of the index more extensive than others. For instance, all articles in *The Daily Herald* index that deal with Utah County news are assigned one or two main subject headings. However, because *The Daily Herald* is Provo City's main newspaper, every article dealing with Provo City is indexed completely, using all names and all possible subject headings.

Your scope may differ from the sample index, but be sure to indicate both what is included and what is not included when writing the scope. As you begin indexing, refer to the scope frequently to ensure consistency.

Remember that the scope is also determined by the source and level of funding. If your local newspaper office is paying for the indexing service, it can be tailored to the newspaper's needs. For example, the staff might find it useful to have all of their local columnists, feature editors, and photographers indexed by name. This extra work may give the newspaper all the reasons it needs to fund your indexing.

2

Subject Headings

LIBRARY OF CONGRESS SUBJECT HEADINGS

Indexers should use the latest edition of *Library of Congress Subject Headings,* which can be found in most libraries, to determine what subject heading is appropriate. However, many local topics cannot be found in *LCSH,* and it is therefore up to the indexer to assign a consistent heading:

```
HOFFMAN BOMBINGS

LAFFERTY MURDERS

MULTIPLE SCLEROSIS WALKATHON
```

To write your own subject headings, do a keyword search on the Online Public Access Catalog (OPAC) at your local library to find subjects and headings similar to those you wish to use. To do this, pull up an index of titles on the OPAC. Pick the one closest to your subject and enter its number. When the screen displays the details of your selection, look for the subject heading, which will be in Library of Congress Subject Heading format. Add it to your customized Subject Authority File, which can be found in appendix B and on the disk (filenames subafwp.doc for WordPerfect users and subafmsw.doc for Microsoft Word users).

STYLING GUIDELINES

Subentries

Subentries, topics that can be found under a more general heading, are indicated with a dash (two hyphens). For example, there are several subentries under the subject heading WATER: WATER—POLLUTION; WATER—STORAGE; and WATER—SUPPLY.

Capitalization Guidelines

Subject headings should be styled using only capital letters to avoid inconsistencies in alphabetizing and eliminate judgment calls in applying rules of capitalization.

Punctuation Guidelines for Indexing Government and School Subject Headings

Most index terms consist of a single word or a name. However, when a term is complicated or has several components, as is the case with government entities and the names and departments of schools and universities, the indexer must decide on consistent styling. Such complex entries found in the Provo *Daily Herald* indexing project are styled as follows.

Government Entities

The jurisdiction of the government entity comes first, followed by a period:

```
UTAH. AIR QUALITY, DIVISION OF
UTAH. RECLAMATION, BUREAU OF
PROVO. POLICE DEPARTMENT
PROVO. MUNICIPAL COUNCIL
```

Unfortunately, government subject headings are not always this clear-cut. For instance, Provo's Chamber of Commerce has combined with Orem's Chamber of Commerce. All newspaper articles refer to Provo/Orem Chamber of Commerce. How should the subject heading for this body be styled? One solution is PROVO OREM CHAMBER OF COMMERCE, which is easier than the alternative subject headings:

```
PROVO. COMMERCE, CHAMBER OF
OREM. COMMERCE, CHAMBER OF
```

This example demonstrates the importance of having a consistent indexer or indexing team to decide on problematic subject headings.

Schools and Universities

For schools and universities, the name of the institution comes first, followed by a period. The specific division of the school follows. For example:

```
USU. BIG BLUE CLUB
PROVO HIGH SCHOOL. THEATRE DEPT.
```

The indexer must decide on a consistent way of styling university departments and colleges. For instance:

```
USU. AGRICULTURE, COLLEGE OF
USU. GEOLOGY, DEPT. OF
```

rather than

```
USU. AGRICULTURE, COLLEGE OF
USU. DEPARTMENT OF GEOLOGY
```

Subentries vs. Government and School Subject Headings

Sometimes it can be difficult to determine whether a complex term should be its own entry or a subtopic of another term. For example, note the following entries:

```
GARFIELD HIGH SCHOOL—DRAMA
GARFIELD HIGH SCHOOL. THEATRE, DEPT. OF
```

These subject headings are very close in theme. However, the first example would be used to index dramatic events that happened at or were sponsored by Garfield High School. The second example would be used only to index stories about the department itself, such as the administration or policies of Garfield High School's Theatre Department. This can be a fine distinction, but with practice an indexer can become comfortable making the call.

The indexer will use dashes when referring to broader terms in connection with a government agency, school, or university. For example:

```
PROVO—BUDGET
UTAH—LEGISLATURE
```

Dashes are used in all sports and theater entries unless the article refers to the athletic department or theater department. For instance:

```
USU. ATHLETICS, DEPT. OF
USU—FOOTBALL
PROVO HIGH SCHOOL—BASEBALL
```

and

```
USU. THEATRE, DEPT. OF
(When the theater department is mentioned by name.)
USU—THEATRE
(When the article refers to a specific production, in which
case the name of the production should also be indexed:
e.g., FIDDLER ON THE ROOF.)
```

When the computer alphabetizes (sorts) all the entries, the subject headings without periods or dashes will be listed first. Second come the subject headings followed by a period, and last of all, the subject headings followed by dashes.

CROSS-REFERENCING SUBJECT HEADINGS

The extent to which an article will be indexed is determined by the scope of the index. Always keep in mind the patron who will be using the index as you consider which subject headings might need cross-references. For example, a patron might look up articles on Provo's budget either under PROVO—BUDGET or under BUDGET—PROVO, so index the article both ways.

SUBJECT HEADINGS
FOR NEWSPAPER ELEMENTS

Editorials and Letters to the Editor

Many editorials and letters to the editor from local citizens may deal with subjects not included in the scope, such as solutions to world problems. In these cases, index under the name of the writer only. For example, a letter to the editor titled "Stop Hunger in Africa" by Mitzi Anderson would be indexed as follows:

```
Subject Heading    Headline/Summary
ANDERSON, MITZI    STOP HUNGER IN AFRICA. EDITORIAL
```

By ending the headline/summary with ". EDITORIAL," the patron using the index can distinguish factual information from opinions.

Photographs

Photographs are a vital part of a community's history. If an article is accompanied by a photo, the summary must always end with ". PHOTO." If the scope permits, you may choose to include the name of the photographer. This would give an additional access point to the news article.

Articles

Article headlines may not always contain the information a researcher might expect to find when searching for the story. Worse yet, some headlines can even be misleading. Let's examine a typical newspaper article:

Snow is coming!

Fred Snow will be the new football coach at Lincoln High School, it was announced today. Snow replaces Marty Zumac, who left to be head coach at Central Community College in Elm City. "It is exciting to be a part of the Lincoln Lion tradition," said Coach Snow. "I'm predicting a winning season for the first time in the history of the school." Snow comes with impressive credentials. As an assistant coach in Topeka, he helped guide the Coolidge Tigers to an eight and five season after several losing seasons. He also enjoys working with young men and teaching them the principles of quality football strategy. Principal John Gordon expressed confidence that with some technical help in the coaching area, the Lions might just have their best year ever. Ace Mattell, the starting quarterback, was enthusiastic, too. "I respect Snow's background as an offensive coach. A solid offense is just what the doctor ordered." The public is invited to meet Coach Snow at an open house to be held on Saturday, August 21, 1994, at the High School gymnasium.

The first thing you notice is the story's headline. A good newspaper headline writer will name key elements of the article in a concise fashion. This headline did not. You should therefore change the index headline/summary to improve clarity and help the researcher looking for the story:

FRED SNOW NEW HEAD FOOTBALL COACH AT CENTRAL HIGH SCHOOL

The indexer must also be familiar with the inverted style of newspaper writing. In this style, all important information is provided in the first paragraph. The classic newspaper questions of Who? What? When? Where? Why? and How? are answered in the first few sentences. Even so, do not assume that all the subject matter for indexing is found in the first paragraph. You still will need to scan the entire article for other names and references to index, scope permitting.

Depending on the scope, you may assign one main subject heading to the whole article. However, you will produce a better index by also indexing the key names mentioned in the article. In the preceding example, the main subject heading would be

```
CENTRAL HIGH SCHOOL—FOOTBALL
```

To elaborate, you would add the following subject headings (and other subject headings, depending on your scope):

```
SNOW, FRED

GORDON, JOHN

MATTELL, ACE
```

Once you decide on the subject headings, the remaining data to be entered is fairly self-explanatory. The date, expressed as a number in month/day/year order (01-05-93 for January 5, 1993), is followed by the newspaper section letter, the page number (for single digits, use a two-digit page number: 06 for page 6), and the single-digit column number. Following is an example of how this might appear:

```
Subject
Heading        Date       Sc  Pg  Cl  Headline Summary

SNOW, FRED     01-05-93   D   06  1   FRED SNOW NEW HEAD FOOTBALL COACH AT CENTRAL HS

GORDON, JOHN   01-05-93   D   06  1   FRED SNOW NEW HEAD FOOTBALL COACH AT CENTRAL HS

MATTEL, ACE    01-05-93   D   06  1   FRED SNOW NEW HEAD FOOTBALL COACH AT CENTRAL HS
```

The column number can be tricky. It assumes that the newspaper is indeed printed in newspaper column format. However, some layouts make column identification difficult. In such cases, you must determine how many columns the newspaper format usually contains and, using the top of the newspaper page as a guide, locate the approximate column position over the article. Enter that column number in the column heading.

The headline/summary is generally the headline of the newspaper article, but as with the subject heading, there are exceptions when the headline is not descriptive enough or is even misleading. See comments and examples in chapter 4 on indexing samples.

3

Techniques for Indexing

CONSISTENCY

The secret to a useful index is consistency. Whether the indexing project is undertaken by the staff or by volunteers, it is best for one person to prepare the index (or at least direct the process), because judgment calls will arise, and critical decisions will be more consistent if they are made by a single individual. Unfortunately, this is not always possible, so it is vital for those working on the index to communicate frequently.

One example of why communication and consistency are so important is that discrepancies often arise in how the names of frequent newsmakers appear. For instance, if you have a local newsmaker named Jonathan P. Winkle, he might be referred to in news stories as Jonathan P. Winkle, John Winkle, Jonathan Winkle, or J. P. Winkle. For indexing purposes, one form of his name must be chosen; otherwise, confusion will result. For example, if the newsmaker is referred to as John Winkle in some stories and Jonathan Winkle in others, when the index is sorted, the John Winkle references will precede the Jonathan Winkle references, and the dates of the articles will be out of order.

In selecting a name form, it is generally safest to use the name the person goes by in the community. You may cross-reference this name with any other vastly different names by which the person is known. Keep a card file on prominent names in the community and how they are indexed. (Hint: If there is any question about how to refer to a person in the index, check the phone book or simply call the individual and ask. This is not time-consuming and makes for a better index.)

Consistency of subject headings is also crucial, and *Library of Congress Subject Headings* will be an important resource. In addition, your state may have published a work that helps indexers with subject headings. In Utah, the Library Association's Steering Committee on Newspaper Indexing prepared a manual titled *Guidelines for Indexing Utah's Newspapers*. This volume serves as an arbitrator of headlines, particularly as found in Utah.

USING MICROFILM

Much of your indexing may be done from microfilm, which is more difficult to work with than a hard copy of a newspaper. The problem is keeping your place.

Joy T. Horton and Richard W. Horton of Vernal, Utah, are currently indexing *The Vernal Express* from 1891 to the present, using microfilm. They suggest using two people to index microfilm. One person enters data into the computer while the other focuses on the microfilm machine and reads the indexing data out loud. The microfilm reader scans the page from left to right, keeping track of the column position. For stories that continue on a later page, once the story has been indexed, the microfilm reader must remember to return to the page on which the article began. Otherwise, it is possible to skip pages of news articles.

If you have any say in how the microfilm is formatted, chose microfilm that produces a positive image, or dark letters on white background. White letters on black background are harder to read.

INDEXING COMPLEX SUBJECT MATTER

An organization that has a single purpose or does not appear frequently in the news can often be indexed under a subject heading without subdivisions. However, some organizations generate a great deal of news in a variety of areas. Subject headings for these institutions should be subdivided; otherwise, the patron ends up combing through a myriad of information, much of which is totally irrelevant to the topic being researched.

For example, imagine the frustration of a researcher who is looking for a story on your local high school's drama club and must read through several lines of headings that also include football games, basketball games, honor rolls, and so on. This is where subject heading subdivisions (properly punctuated with periods and dashes) become useful. When sorted, the newly subdivided data would appear as follows:

```
PROVO HIGH SCHOOL                  11-01-91 B 06 1
PROVO HIGH SCHOOL. DRAMA CLUB      11-15-91 A 07 2
PROVO HIGH SCHOOL—DRAMA            11-03-91 C 02 1
PROVO HIGH SCHOOL—FOOTBALL         11-02-91 B 02 1
PROVO HIGH SCHOOL—FOOTBALL         11-26-91 D 02 3
PROVO HIGH SCHOOL—HONORS           11-24-91 D 02 2
PROVO HIGH SCHOOL—VOLLEYBALL       11-07-91 E 05 1
PROVO HIGH SCHOOL—VOLLEYBALL       11-10-91 H 07 1
```

Of course, if your subject matter is general enough, then the high school can and should appear without a subdivision, as in the first entry in the preceding list.

The same need for subject heading subdivisions is found in government index listings. As you can see, government listings can be quite diverse:

```
PROVO. ART BOARD                        11-29-91 D 07 3
PROVO. ARTS COUNCIL                     11-10-91 C 07 1
PROVO. ARTS COUNCIL                     11-28-91 F 05 5
PROVO. CEMETERY                         11-08-91 B 01 3
PROVO. CEMETERY                         11-15-91 B 04 1
PROVO. CITY COUNCIL                     11-01-91 B 04 2
PROVO. CITY COUNCIL                     11-04-91 C 01 3
PROVO. ENERGY DEPT.                     11-26-91 A 01 5
PROVO. LIBRARY                          11-02-91 C 02 5
PROVO. LIBRARY                          11-09-91 C 02 5
PROVO. LIBRARY                          11-23-91 D 02 5
PROVO. LIBRARY                          11-30-91 D 02 5
PROVO. MUNICIPAL AIRPORT                11-11-91 A 01 1
PROVO. MUNICIPAL COUNCIL                11-06-91 A 01 5
PROVO. MUNICIPAL COUNCIL—MEETINGS       11-13-91 A 01 1
PROVO. PLANNING COMMISSION              11-14-91 D 01 5
PROVO. POLICE DEPT.                     11-17-91 A 01 6
PROVO—LAND                              11-27-91 B 01 4
PROVO—LAWSUITS                          11-22-91 B 01 1
```

CORRECTING QUIRKY PROBLEMS

Even after the best proofing job, problems may still show up. To help resolve them, be sure to keep your newspapers (in order of date) until after the monthly index you have been working on is printed. Following are some examples of the quirky indexing problems you might encounter.

After your sort is completed, you might find two very similar entries:

```
HOSKINS, JERRY   11-03-92 A 01 03   BAGS BIG BUCK. PHOTO
HOSKINS, GERI    11-03-92 A 01 03   BAGS BIG BUCK. PHOTO
```

The question is, is this a duplication with a misspelling of the first name, or, in fact, were both Geri and Jerry in the picture? If you have the old newspaper, you can find out for sure.

Another quirk is the double entry. Sometimes an entry is duplicated, and you will not realize it until after sorting. When you see what appears to be a double entry, be aware that your computer monitor may not be displaying the entire line. To check, place your cursor on the line in question and hit (End). This will take your cursor to the extreme right of that line, and you can see whether the possible duplicate entry is, for instance, a photo. The following example demonstrates the problem:

```
DOE, JOHN    11-01-91 B 05 1 ELK RIDGE RESIDENTS CAN SELECT
DOE, JOHN    11-01-91 B 06 1 ELK RIDGE RESIDENTS CAN SELECT
```

Looks like a possible duplication, doesn't it? But put the cursor on the second line and hit (End), and you'll see that they are in fact on different pages and that one reference is for the photo:

```
11-01-91 B 05 1 ELK RIDGE RESIDENTS CAN SELECT FROM SIX
11-01-91 B 06 1 ELK RIDGE RESIDENTS CAN SELECT FROM SIX. PHOTO
```

4

Indexing Samples That Illustrate How to Handle Various Situations

As you begin indexing articles, you may come up against complex, confusing, or unfamiliar situations. Following is a series of suggestions illustrated with actual articles, subject headings, and headline/summaries for handling these situations.

HEADLINES

Headlines That Are Too Long

Headlines may need to be shortened to fit the headline/summary. You can add to or change the headline to make a better headline/summary statement. Following are examples of two different summaries for the article " 'Amen' Question Stumps Many Religious Scholars":

Subject Heading	Date	Sc	Pg	Cl	Headline/Summary
RELIGION	07-17-94	E	2	1	'AMEN' QUESTION STUMPS SCHOLARS
RELIGION	07-17-94	E	2	1	'AMEN' QUESTION STUMPS MANY RELIGIOUS SCHOLARS

'Amen' Question Stumps Many Religious Scholars

Question: "Amen" is most frequently used in the Bible at the end of a phrase, as a kind of confirmation of what has been said. Why did Jesus sometimes use "Amen" as an introductory term?

Answer: According to the *Anchor Bible Dictionary* (Doubleday, 1992), this question has bedeviled scholars for years.

One such scholar was Joachim Jeremias, who argued that Jesus employed well-known language in a radically fresh way as a way to assert in advance the authority of his pronouncements.

Others have argued, however, that there was some precedent prior to Jesus for the introductory "Amen."

And still others have argued that the use of the Hebrew "Amen" among early Hellenistic Christian communities was taken up to mark the faithful transmission of tradition from Judaism to Christianity.

Something of a consensus exists that the introductory phrase "in truth"—spoken in Aramaic, the language used by Jesus and those of the early church—was transformed into "Amen."

That added weight to the authority of Jesus's sayings and conveyed the theological conviction that the one who spoke was sufficiently credible to be called "the Amen."

No Headline or Misleading Headline

Rewrite the headline/summary so that it better reflects each subject heading and can easily be copied with a macro or with a software copying feature.

Gary Stewart

Dynix has appointed Gary Stewart as manager of implementation services. Stewart replaces Kevin Ash, who was recently promoted to general manager of Dynix Marquis. Stewart will be responsible for the delivery of products and services including training, data conversions and migrations, network designs, and library consulting services.

Subject Heading	*Headline/Summary*
STEWART, GARY	STEWART APPOINTED AS DYNIX IMPLEMENTATION MANAGER. PHOTO
DYNIX, INC.	STEWART APPOINTED AS DYNIX IMPLEMENTATION MANAGER. PHOTO

Incomplete Headline

Sometimes the headline/summary should include more than the newspaper headline to provide a better description, as with letters to the editor.

Letters

Opts to Pass

Editor:
    I have been watching with interest the general fuss over whether we [Latter-Day Saints] should ignore the "R" rating and see *Shindler's List* because of its moving representation of the Holocaust.

Memories of that monumental example of man's inhumanity to man should never be lost. However, the issue for me is whether or not I should go to any "R"-rated movie, and if I leave *Shindler's List* off my list, am I somehow morally deficient.

Practicing Latter-Day Saints (I will keep practicing until I get it right) have been instructed to not go to "R"-rated movies.

I know the rating system is stupid. Many "PG-13" movies ought to be "R," and some "R" movies ought to be "PG-13," and some "PG's" are corrupt. In this confusion, my only clear guideline is to follow the brethren—no "R"-rated movies.

With this inflexible standard I might occasionally miss out on an inspiring movie, but I am prepared to run that risk.

I understand that *Shindler's List* has some graphic nudity and sex that didn't make a point about the Holocaust, but perhaps overall, it might have been a positive experience. However, at the risk of occasionally missing out, I don't want to spend my time in a dumpster looking for an occasional lost piece of jewelry.

Wading through all that garbage in hopes of occasionally finding something worthwhile is not a good use of my time.

For those who were touched by *Shindler's List,* that's fine. I'll pass. Maybe I'll read the book.

Howard J. Ruff
Springville

Because the title of this article doesn't provide enough information to make a complete summary, further information must be added, as in the following examples:

Subject Heading	*Headline/Summary*
RUFF, HOWARD	OPTS TO PASS ON *SHINDLER'S LIST*. EDITORIAL
SHINDLER'S LIST	OPTS TO PASS ON *SHINDLER'S LIST*. EDITORIAL

LOCAL ANNOUNCEMENTS

Wedding and Anniversary Announcements

For wedding and anniversary announcements, use both names in the headline/summary:

Annette Carlton
Glenn McIntosh

Carlton, McIntosh

Annette Carlton, daughter of Ken and Lorene Carlton of Lehi, will marry Glenn McIntosh, son of Robert and Carol McIntosh of Burlington, Wyoming, on Saturday, April 16, in the Salt Lake LDS Temple. A reception will honor the couple that evening from 7-9 at the LDS Church at 145 E. 1500 North, Lehi. The bride-to-be graduated from Lehi High School, attended Dixie College, and is a student at Utah Valley State College majoring in elementary education. She works at Provo Title and Escrow. Her fiancé graduated from high school in Burlington and is a student at Brigham Young University majoring in accounting. Bridal attendants are Brenda Pulley, Linda Olsen, Janae Anderson, Natalie Clark, and Jamie Carlton.

```
Subject Heading       Headline/Summary
CARLTON, ANNETTE    CARLTON AND MCINTOSH TO WED. PHOTO
MCINTOSH, GLENN     CARLTON AND MCINTOSH TO WED. PHOTO
```

Obituaries

When indexing obituaries, use the individual's full name, and be sure to mention the photo, if any.

Norma Eddy Bird

Norma Eddy Bird, age 90, of Springville, died Sunday, May 8, 1994, in Springville.

She was born November 28, 1903, in Spanish Fork to Jane Bigley Eddy. She married Guy H. Bird April 10, 1923, in Provo.

She was a member of the LDS Church and had been Young Women's President and a visiting teacher. She had been employed at Jack's Toggery in Springville for many years. She enjoyed gardening, her grandchildren, classical music, flowers, and crocheting.

She is survived by three sons: N. Guy Bird and wife Louise of Santa Clara, Utah; Robert J. Bird and wife Rowene and John O. Bird and wife Colleen of Springville; 14 grandchildren; 37 great-grandchildren; 5 great-great-grandchildren. She was preceded in death by one son, LaRay.

Funeral will be Wednesday at 11 a.m. in the Wheeler Mortuary Chapel, 211 E. 200 South Springville. Friends may call one hour prior to services. Burial will be in the Springville Evergreen Cemetery.

```
Subject Heading            Headline/Summary
BIRD, NORMA EDDY           OBITUARY. PHOTO
```

EDITORIALS AND LETTERS TO THE EDITOR

Guidelines for Indexing Editorials and Letters to the Editor

1. Always add ". EDITORIAL" after the headline/summary to distinguish opinion from fact.

2. Many editorials have no clear-cut subject matter. They can be indexed under the author's name.

3. Some editorials have been assigned catchy headlines that need more explanation in the headline/summary.

```
                   Letters
```

Irresponsible

```
Editor:

    Irresponsible off-road use is one of the
major causes of closure of areas for special-
interest uses. Special-interest groups call
others with differing recreational pursuits
or views "elite" but would never consider
themselves as such.
    It is true irony when a group like the
Utah Trail Machine Association goes around
calling others the names they do when the
names fit themselves so perfectly. If you
are not part of the solution, you are part
of the problem.
    Throwing verbal rocks at others solves
nothing but does create greater rifts. It
is total subjectivity.
    And may I remind them that we all pay
for abuse and degradation to our watershed,
the lifeblood of our desert homes.

Brent Mortensen
Orem
```

Following is a list of three possible subject headings and a headline/summary for the above editorial.

Subject Heading	Headline/Summary
MORTENSEN, BRENT	OFF-ROAD VEHICLES IRRESPONSIBLE. EDITORIAL
ALL-TERRAIN VEHICLES	OFF-ROAD VEHICLES IRRESPONSIBLE. EDITORIAL
UTAH TRAIL MACH. ASSOC.	VEHICLES IRRESPONSIBLE. EDITORIAL

Editorials About World and National Issues by Local Residents

Many local residents give opinions on world and national affairs. These editorials should be listed under the author's name even if world and national affairs are not part of the index scope.

Letters

Legal luxuries

Editor:

The front page of the June 29 *Daily Herald* carried a story confirming that President Clinton will be setting up a legal defense fund to assist him in paying his attorney's fees for private legal actions arising before he became president. The writer quotes several experts as saying the legal fund is the best solution to a bad situation. The story goes on to say that President Clinton's legal bills might be $2 million, more than even the president can afford.

I would suggest that there is a better solution. If Mr. Clinton cannot afford the most high-priced legal talent in the country, perhaps he should hire an attorney that he can afford. Most of my clients would love to have someone else pay their attorney's fees. Instead, most of them have to settle for the legal services that they can afford. I would love to practice law only in behalf of clients who were very wealthy and could afford the best of everything. Instead, I

must give them what services we both feel
are realistically necessary and appropriate
under the circumstances.

The president's idea of spending money
on attorneys that he cannot afford is simply
another symptom of the disease that we all
know affects Washington bureaucrats. If Mr.
Clinton were to rethink his legal strategy
in this instance, it might be a signal that we
finally found a president who understands
reality. Unfortunately, that will not happen.

It is a sad fact that only the wealthy,
and the poor who are eligible for public
subsidized legal services, can afford all
the legal services that they desire. The
middle class must do with less. Wouldn't it
be nice if our leaders for once set a good
example?

W. Andrew McCullough
Orem

Subject Heading	*Headline/Summary*
MCCULLOUGH, W. ANDREW	CLINTON'S LEGAL LUXURIES. EDITORIAL

ADVERTISEMENTS

Although they are not usually indexed, you should index an advertisement
that contains a named photograph or might be of historical interest.

Successfully Serving My Family for Four Generations

Richard J. Baker, H.I.S.

. . . That is why I choose to join the
Littlefield Company. I have found that my
33 years of personal experience in wearing
hearing aids has benefited our customers
greatly.

Littlefield's has the experience you
trust and expect in servicing all your

hearing needs. Littlefield's is the oldest hearing instrument dispensary in Utah.

Littlefield's was the first dispensary in the United States to successfully assemble and service hearing aids in their office.

Why we choose to manufacture our own hearing aids:

- To provide the best and fastest service available.

- Give each order personal attention.

- Be in total control of each fitting and maintain quality control.

- Incorporate new developments immediately.

- Utilize our own vast experience.

- Provide the most advanced, highest QUALITY AIDS AT A LOWER PRICE.

Littlefield's
Since 1948
*"Call us for a free hear-
ing evaluation."*
PROVO
424 N. Freedom Blvd.
373-7989

Richard J. Baker,
H.I.S.

Subject Heading	Headline/Summary
BAKER, RICHARD, H.I.S.	FOUR GENERATIONS AT LITTLEFIELD'S. PHOTO
LITTLEFIELD'S	FOUR GENERATIONS AT LITTLEFIELD'S. PHOTO

REVIEWS

Index reviews that fall outside the local scope if they are written by local reviewers. For example, even though the following musical review is beyond the local scope, Christi Conover is a local reviewer and should be indexed. At the end of the headline/summary, put ". REVIEW" in the same way that you would use ". PHOTO" and ". EDITORIAL."

Madonna's contribution is a highlight of soundtrack

With Honors/Motion Picture Soundtrack
Various Artists
Warner Brothers
Grade: B+

Despite what your current image of Madonna may be, the fact remains that earlier in her career she released some great songs. However, her work lately has been quite disappointing.

This emphasizes how refreshing it is to hear the gentle but rhythmic and definitely pretty "I'll Remember," Madonna's contribution to the soundtrack of the new movie *With Honors*.

Congratulations to this artist for performing this song with sensitivity and warmth. It is a highlight of this disc. With lyrics such as, "I'll remember the love that you gave me, now that I'm standing on my own. I'll remember the way that you changed me. I'll remember. . . ," this song could be an anthem for graduating seniors everywhere.

The remainder of this disc incorporates talents of artists new and old. The Cult contributes a mix of its guitar-driven "She Sells Sanctuary," a sure winner in any context. Duran Duran offers the slow "Thank You" with its gentle guitar strumming—a song that may not be the band's best work but is pleasing nonetheless. The Pretenders perform a pretty song called "Forever Young" that matches the quality of their hits.

The band Belly offers a bouncy, fun song in "It's Not Unusual," and Candlebox continues the grunge tradition with "Cover Me."

Things slow down a bit for Grant Lee Buffalo's "Fuzzy," a rather boring and ponderous piece, while Babble's "Tribe" lacks spirit as well. The keyboard and guitar in Mudhoney's contribution, "Run S---head, Run," overpower the vocals.

Some interesting variety is added at the end of the album: Lindsey Buckingham's "On the Wrong Side" has a Gaelic feel to it, and Lyle Lovett's "Blue Skies" is performed by an intimate jazz combo with string bass and piano.

Overall this album is an interesting combination of styles and bands. The few songs that fall short can be overlooked for the majority of the songs that are well done.

The following sample index demonstrates how the previous review would be indexed. Notice that the headline alone is insufficient as a summary and should be rewritten to accurately reflect the subject of the review.

Subject Heading	*Headline/Summary*
CONOVER, CHRISTI	MADONNA HIGHLIGHT OF *WITH HONORS* SOUNDTRACK. REVIEW

5

Preparing to Index Using Word-Processing Software

LOOKING AHEAD TO THE
FINAL INDEX PRODUCT

The index that you will be creating on your personal computer will be printed in landscape fashion to include the most information possible per line (when you select the landscape orientation, it is the long sides of the piece of paper that become the top and bottom of the page). In addition, each entry must be on a single line. If the word processor wraps a headline/summary entry to the next line, you must delete inconsequential words so that the headline/summary fits on the first line; otherwise, the alphanumeric sorting process will not work.

You will need to create a three-line header for the top of each page. The first line of the header indicates that the index is a newspaper index. This line also includes the name of the newspaper, the month, and the year. The second line is blank. The third line displays category heads for the information that will be included in each entry: Subject Heading (newsmaker, Library of Congress subject heading, cross-reference), Date (date of newspaper), Sc (section of the paper, expressed alphabetically), Pg (page number, expressed in two digits), Cl (column number, counted from left to right and expressed as a single digit), and Headline/Summary (headline of the story, sometimes altered for clarity).

The index is prepared monthly and kept in a three-ring binder with tabs for each month. Pages should be printed on both sides and inserted into the binder in such a manner that (1) each two-page spread forms a continuous list and (2) when the pages are turned, the reader does not have to turn the binder to find the top of the list.

Once a year, if the library desires, an annual summary can be prepared from the monthly diskettes. To do a sorting project of this magnitude, you must have, or have access to, a computer with plenty of free memory. Even though a year's indexing amounts to perhaps 35K, additional free space is needed for the sorting process. To create an annual document, all 12 diskettes of indexing are retrieved into the same document and then sorted alphanumerically as described in the section *Sorting the Index into Alphanumeric Order* that appears in each disk file (you may also want to create semiannual documents). The annual printout then replaces the month-by-month indexes in the three-ring binder for that particular year. Your patrons may prefer to do a word search using the index disk rather than look through the hard copy. Approximately six months of indexing will fit on a 3.5" disk, depending on the scope of the index.

SETTING UP YOUR
WORD-PROCESSING PROGRAM
FOR NEWSPAPER INDEXING

Examine the files on the disk that was enclosed with this book. These chapters are tailored to your particular edition of WordPerfect or Microsoft Word and will help you prepare your index. Choose the chapter that matches your software, print it out, read it, and keep the printout for your reference. Note that each disk chapter contains a sample index for the particular software program. The disk contains files for the following programs:

WordPerfect 5.0 and 5.1 for DOS—filename: wp501dos.doc

WordPerfect 6.0 for Windows—filename: wp60win.doc

WordPerfect 6.1 for Windows—filename: wp61win.doc

Microsoft Word 2.0 for Windows—filename: msw20win.doc

Microsoft Word 6.0 for Windows—filename: msw60win.doc

Shortcut Opportunity

If you are familiar with your word-processing software, you can save some time by formatting your screen as follows:

Select landscape orientation (11" x 8.5")

Turn left justification on

Set top and bottom margins to 0.8"

Set left and right margins for 0.25"

Set tab orientation from the left edge of the paper (instead of from the left margin)

Clear all tabs and reset at 4", 4.9", 5.2", 5.5", and 5.8"

Set page numbers to appear in the top right corner

If you can easily perform these tasks, you are ready to skip ahead in the appropriate software chapter to the information on setting up a header.

A

Getting Funding for Your Indexing Project

Once you have learned how to index, the next step is to obtain funding for your indexing project. Remember that the extent of the scope will determine the staff time, materials, and cost. Be sure to calculate your costs carefully. If your figures are too low, you may find yourself permanently shortchanged; if your figures are too high, no one will be able to afford to fund the project.

As you calculate your costs, you will need to determine two things. First, what do you need to be paid — the same amount of money as your regular job, more money than your regular job, or are you willing to do it for less? Determine your desired price range, then run some sample calculations based on the high and low figures. Second, do you wish to be paid per hour or per paper? If you choose to be paid per paper, remember that some issues of the paper are much more time-consuming than others. The Provo *Daily Herald*'s Sunday edition and Thursday edition are surprisingly large, whereas the Monday and Friday papers are a bit sparse. Thus, if you chose to be paid per paper, calculate the average number of hours it takes to index the paper. For example:

Sunday paper = 2 hours x hourly rate = Sunday billing

Friday paper = .5 hours x hourly rate = Friday billing

If you choose to be paid hourly, the calculation would be

(hourly rate x average number of hours per paper x 30.4 [average number of days in a month]) + cost of materials = $ monthly billing

The materials you will need are white $8\frac{1}{2}$-x-11" paper for your printer, diskettes to store monthly indexes, and printer supplies such as toner cartridges, ribbon, ink cartridges, and so on. These are the basics. If you choose to amortize the cost of a desktop computer, stationery, and other overhead business expenses, you may, of course, do so. However, you must remain competitively priced.

Let's assume that you have finished your scope, completed your calculations, and determined that you need to be paid $500 per month (or $6,000 annually) for this service, everything included. How, then, do you go about finding funding?

The first step is to ask the question, Who will benefit the most from having an index of the local newspaper? Some possible candidates might be the newspaper itself, the city government, major businesses, historical societies, prominent individuals, and private foundations or trusts. A brainstorming session may help you come up with many others.

The next step is to list the candidates in order of their likelihood to fund your project. Then recruit the highest authority possible to contact potential sponsors and present your proposal. If it is the library director, great; if it is the mayor, even better! But make sure that whoever you choose to represent you is conversant about newspaper indexing and why it is important.

Write up a proposal for funding. One option to be considered is the plausibility of doing a retrospective index. By indexing back in time as well as keeping current, the historical value of the index grows dramatically, and a good case can be made for funding such a venture. Next, have your representative set up a meeting to present the proposal to the highest authority available in your target organization.

Once you obtain funding, look for ways to turn your indexing project into a line item in your funding source's budget. Obtaining funding for your indexing project on an annual basis becomes dramatically easier when your project is a line item in a budget for expenditures.

Following is a sample proposal. Note that the background information is personalized and applicable to Provo, Utah, only. You will need to adapt it to your own situation.

A PROPOSAL FOR NEWSPAPER INDEXING

[your name here]

Prepared especially for

[name of target sponsor]

NEWSPAPER INDEXING—A PROPOSAL

[Sample only. Revise to meet your specific needs]

BACKGROUND:

[Provide some background information about your library and the needs of its patrons. Then show why an indexing service is important to the success of the library.]

As a reference librarian for the Provo City Library, I found it a challenge to research the 20,000 questions our department encountered each year. A significant number of these questions concerned local events and personalities usually reported in the newspaper. Many times, the local newspaper is the only place where this information can be found.

Newspapers, small or large, constitute a great wealth of historical information for the communities they serve. Researchers, historians, and genealogists of today—as well as tomorrow—can be well served by a newspaper index.

How the Provo City Library came to index its newspaper is an interesting story. Provo, Utah, has one of the highest birth rates in the nation. *The Daily Herald* publishes birth announcements at random. Young mothers would sit at a microfilm machine for hours attempting to locate these records. In addition, in the early 1980s, the library began receiving inquiries from across the nation about local newspaper articles on Gary Gilmore. All we had at that time was a clipping file that was messy and subject to theft. The idea for a newspaper index was born, and the index itself began in 1982, facilitating research for local patrons and others. We indexed on the Apple, using Sears subject headings.

In July of 1988, we began using the *Guidelines for Indexing Utah's Newspapers* by the ULA Steering Committee on Utah Newspaper Indexing. An IBM program allowed us to expand subject headings and compile comprehensive monthly updates.

THE PROPOSAL

This proposal is to contract with [your name] to index [name of local newspaper]. The indexing would use Library of Congress subject headings, and its extent would be determined by the scope of the index. The scope might include all news articles on city/county levels, including community colleges and universities. More specifically, it might include the following categories:

1. Biographical stories: birth, engagement, wedding announcements, and obituaries

2. Business

3. Sports

4. Photos and editorials

The extent of the scope will, of course, determine the amount of indexing required and, in turn, its cost.

IN RETURN FOR INDEXING SERVICES

1. [Your name] will receive a complimentary newspaper subscription sent to [his/her] home.

2. A monthly fee of $ [your fee] would be paid to [your name].

3. Should the library seek other funding for the index, the library will act as agent, paying [your name] in full and collecting from other funding entities.

IT IS THEREFORE PROPOSED . . .

. . . that [your name] be officially assigned to the work of indexing [name of newspaper], beginning [date] at the rate of $ [your fee] per month.

To these terms we mutually agree, as indicated by our signatures below, on this date, _____.

_____   _____

Name of your library   Name of newspaper

_____   _____

Your name   Sponsor's name

From *How to Index Your Local Newspaper.* © 1995. Libraries Unlimited. (800) 237-6124.

B

Subject
Authority File

HOW TO USE THE
SUBJECT AUTHORITY FILE

The following subject authority file will help you choose consistent subject headings as you index your newspaper. For example, if you have a story about a local kidnapping, do you choose KIDNAPPING or ABDUCTION as the subject heading? If the freeway outside of town will be resurfaced, should your subject heading be HIGHWAY ENGINEERING or ROADS? Actually, in either example, both subject headings could be correct; the point is to use one heading consistently. If it has been a long time since you indexed a similar story, you might forget which subject heading you last used, and two similar stories would end up indexed under two different subject headings. If you are not a librarian, or are just learning about subject headings, the subject authority file can help you determine what an appropriate subject heading might be: for example, is it AGRICULTURAL PRODUCTS or FARM PRODUCE? When you consult the subject authority file, you will see that the correct heading is FARM PRODUCE.

All approved subject headings are formatted in all capital letters. Those subject heads listed with upper and lowercase letters are *not* approved, but a "See" cross-reference will refer you to an acceptable subject heading. "See also" cross-references refer you from one approved subject heading to one or more other approved headings.

This file is not comprehensive. It's designed to provide a basic framework upon which to build a more specific, comprehensive local subject index. The file is double spaced so that as you work with the subject authority file, you can add your own local subject headings (for instance, the correct version of a frequent local newsmaker's name) and make notes on the hard copy to indicate your decisions on particular headings. Better yet, you can call up the subject authority file on the accompanying disk (filenames are subafwp.doc [WordPerfect format] and subafmsw.doc [Microsoft Word format]) and update it as the need arises. An easy way to do this is to split the screen so that your subject authority file is on top and your indexing screen is on the bottom. If you are using a Windows program, you can do this by simply opening both files in your document and using **Window—Tile** if you have WordPerfect or **Windows—Arrange All** if you have Microsoft Word. Simply use your mouse to click between windows whenever you like and make changes to the subject authority file. Use the search function to find your subject heading, but don't forget to use lowercase to enter your search request if your software is case sensitive, which most programs are.

The more you use it, the more valuable your subject authority file will become. Be sure to back it up, as you would all your software files. You would be wise to keep a copy on both the hard drive and a disk, with the disk backing up the hard drive.

THE SUBJECT AUTHORITY FILE

This subject authority file provides a starting point for your own local subject headings file. It was created by Yvonne Stroup at the University of Utah Marriott Library as part of a state-wide project in newspaper indexing, and therefore includes Utah-based subject headings. Ms. Stroup graciously gave us permission to adapt the list for inclusion in this publication. We've removed the Utah-specific headings, but encourage you to add your own local subject headings to the authority file including newsmakers, organizations, and any other Library of Congress headings you find necessary.

ABANDONED CHILDREN

Abandonment of railroad lines

    See

    RAILROADS

ABBEYS

ABDUCTION

    See also

    KIDNAPPING

ABM (ANTIBALLISTIC MISSILES)

ABORTION

ABORTION COUNSELING

ABORTION—MORAL AND ETHICAL ASPECTS

ABORTION—RELIGIOUS ASPECTS

ABRASIVES INDUSTRY

ABSTRACTING AND INDEXING SERVICES

ABUSED CHILDREN

ABUSED WOMEN

ACCIDENTS

    See also subdivision ACCIDENTS under topical subjects, e.g., CONSTRUCTION INDUSTRY—ACCIDENTS; subdivision ACCIDENTS AND INJURIES under individual sports, e.g., SOCCER—ACCIDENTS AND INJURIES; and subdivision INJURIES under individual parts of the body, e.g., FOOT—INJURIES

ACCLIMATIZATION

ACCOUNTING

ACID POLLUTION OF RIVERS, LAKES, ETC.

ACID RAIN

ACOUSTICS

Acquired Immune Deficiency Syndrome

    See

    AIDS (DISEASE)

ACTING

ACTING—AUDITIONS

ACTIONS AND DEFENSES

ACTORS

ACTRESSES

Addiction to drugs

    See

    DRUG ABUSE

ADHESIVES

ADMINISTRATION

ADOBE HOUSES

ADOLESCENT FATHERS

ADOPTION—LAW AND LEGISLATION

ADULT EDUCATION

ADVERTISING

    (May be divided by product being advertised, e.g.:

    ADVERTISING—ALCOHOLIC BEVERAGES

    ADVERTISING—BABY FOODS

    ADVERTISING—DIRECT MAIL)

AERIAL PHOTOGRAPHS

AERIAL SPRAYING AND DUSTING

AERIALISTS

AEROBIC EXERCISES

AERODYNAMICS

    See also

    BALLISTIC MISSILES

AERONAUTICAL CHARTS

AERONAUTICAL ENGINEERS

AERONAUTICAL INSTRUMENTS

AERONAUTICAL LABORATORIES

AERONAUTICAL MUSEUMS

    See also names of specific museums, e.g., HILL AIR FORCE BASE MUSEUM

AERONAUTICAL RESEARCH

AERONAUTICAL SPORTS

    See also

    BALLOON RACING

    SKYDIVING

    PARACHUTING

AERONAUTICS

    See also

    AIRLINES

    AIRPLANES

    AIRPORTS

    ROCKETS

AERONAUTICS—COMMERCIAL

AERONAUTICS—MILITARY

AEROSOLS

AEROSPACE INDUSTRIES

Aerospace weapons systems

    See

    UNITED STATES AIR FORCE—WEAPONS

AEROSTAT SATELLITES

AFFIRMATIVE ACTION PROGRAMS

AFRICAN AMERICANS

AGATES

AGE

AGE AND EMPLOYMENT

AGE DISCRIMINATION

AGED

AGED POLITICIANS

AGED VOLUNTEERS

AGED—ABUSE OF

AGED—CARE AND HYGIENE

AGED—DISEASES

AGED—EMPLOYMENT

AGED—HOME CARE

AGED—SERVICES FOR

AGGREGATE (BUILDING MATERIALS)

AGGRESSIVENESS IN CHILDREN

AGNOSTICISM

AGRICULTURAL ASSISTANCE

AGRICULTURAL LIFE SUPPORTS

AGRICULTURAL MACHINERY

AGRICULTURAL PESTS

AGRICULTURAL PRICE SUPPORTS

AGRICULTURAL PRICES

Agricultural products

    See

    FARM PRODUCE

AGRICULTURAL SURVEYS

AGRICULTURAL SYSTEMS

AGRICULTURAL WAGES

AGRICULTURE

Agriculture laborers—migrant

    See

    MIGRANT LABORERS

AGRICULTURE—ECONOMIC ASPECTS

AIDS (DISEASE)

AIR

AIR ANALYSIS

    See also

    RADIATION

AIR BASES

    See also names of specific bases, e.g., HILL AIR FORCE BASE

Air bases, missile

    See

    GUIDED MISSILE BASES

AIR COMPRESSORS

AIR CONDITIONING

AIR DEFENSE

AIR DEFENSES, CIVIL

Air Force

    See

    UNITED STATES. AIR FORCE

AIR MASSES

    See also

    WEATHER

AIR POLLUTION

AIR POLLUTION CONTROL

AIR POLLUTION CONTROL INDUSTRY

Air ports

    See

    AIRPORTS

AIR RAID SHELTERS

AIR RAID WARNING SYSTEM

    See also

    CIVIL DEFENSE

AIR TRAFFIC CONTROL

AIR TRAVEL

AIR WARFARE

Aircraft noise

    See

    JET PLANES—NOISE

Aircraft, ultralight

    See

    ULTRALIGHT AIRCRAFT

AIRLINES

> See also names of specific airlines, e.g., DELTA AIR LINES

AIRLINES—HIJACKING

AIRPLANE ACCIDENTS

AIRPLANE AMBULANCES

Airplane pilots

> See

> PILOTS

AIRPLANES

AIRPLANES IN POLICE WORK

AIRPLANES, MILITARY

> See also names of specific airplanes, e.g., C-46 MILITARY PLANE

AIRPLANES—ICE PREVENTION

AIRPLANES—JET PROPULSION

AIRPLANES—MODELS

AIRPLANES—NOISE

AIRPORT NOISE

AIRPORT POLICE

AIRPORT ZONING

AIRPORTS

> See also names of specific airports, e.g., CEDAR CITY AIRPORT

AIRPORTS—CONTROL TOWERS

AIRPORTS—LANDING FEES

ALCOHOL

Alcoholic beverage control

> See

> LIQUOR LAWS

ALCOHOLIC BEVERAGES

ALCOHOLICS

ALCOHOLISM

ALCOHOLISM—HOSPITALS

> See also names of specific hospitals, e.g., SAINT MARK'S HOSPITAL
> (SALT LAKE CITY, UTAH)

ALCOHOLISM—TAXATION

ALIEN LABOR

ALIEN LABOR CERTIFICATION

ALIENS

ALIENS, ILLEGAL

ALIMONY

ALKALI INDUSTRY AND TRADE

Allied health personnel

> See

> PARAMEDICS

ALLOYS

> See also names of specific alloys, e.g., ALUMINUM ALLOYS; COPPER ALLOYS

ALL-TERRAIN VEHICLES

ALTITUDES

ALUMINUM

ALUMINUM ALLOYS

ALUMINUM INDUSTRY AND TRADE

ALZHEIMER'S DISEASE

AMATEUR THEATER

AMBULANCE DRIVERS

AMBULANCE SERVICE

> See also

> PARAMEDICS

AMBULANCES

> See also types of ambulances, e.g., AIRPLANE AMBULANCES

American bison

> See

> BUFFALO

AMINO ACIDS

AMMUNITION

    See also

    EXPLOSIVES

AMNESTY

AMPLIFIERS (ELECTRONICS)

AMPLIFIERS—AUDIO

AMPUTATION

AMTRAK

AMUSEMENT PARKS

    See also names of specific amusement parks, e.g., SARATOGA AMUSEMENT PARK

ANASAZI INDIANS

ANATOMY

ANESTHESIA

ANGER

Angina pectoris

    See

    CORONARY HEART DISEASE

ANIMAL CRUELTY

ANIMAL EXPERIMENTATION

ANIMALS

    See also names of specific animals, e.g., BATS; CATS; DOGS

Animals, predatory

    See

    PREDATORY ANIMALS

ANNEXATION

    See also subdivision GROWTH under names of specific towns, e.g., SMITHVILLE—
        GROWTII

ANNUITIES

ANOREXIA

ANTELOPES

    See also

    DEER

ANTENNAS (ELECTRONICS)

ANTHEMS

ANTHROPOLOGY

ANTIBIOTICS

ANTIMISSILE MISSILES

ANTINUCLEAR MOVEMENT

    See also

    NUCLEAR DISARMAMENT

ANTIQUES

ANTISEPTICS

ANTIVENINS

APPETITE DISORDERS

    See also names of specific disorders, e.g., ANOREXIA; BULIMIA

APPLE INDUSTRY

APPORTIONMENT

APPRAISERS

AQUARIUMS

AQUATIC SPORTS

AQUEDUCTS

ARBITRATION, INDUSTRIAL

ARBOR DAY

ARCHAEOLOGY

ARCHERY

ARCHITECTS

ARCHITECTURE

ARCHIVES

ARMED FORCES

    See also specific branches, e.g., UNITED STATES. ARMY

Armistice Day

    See

    VETERANS DAY

ARMS RACE ARRESTS

Army Air Corps

>See

>UNITED STATES. ARMY. AIR CORPS

ARSENIC

ARSON

ART

Art galleries

>See

>ART MUSEUMS

ART MUSEUMS

>See also names of individual museums and galleries

ART—APPRECIATION

>See also

>ART—CRITICISM

ART—AUCTIONS

ART—COMPETITIONS

ART—CRITICISM

ART—DEALERS

ART—EXHIBITIONS

ART—FESTIVALS

>See also names of specific festivals, e.g., OZARK ART FESTIVAL

ART—MUSEUMS

>See also names of specific museums

ART—PRIVATE COLLECTIONS

>See also names of individual collectors

ARTERIES

ARTESIAN WELLS

ARTHRITIS

ARTIFICIAL HEART

Artificial implants

>See

>IMPLANTS, ARTIFICIAL

ARTIFICIAL INSEMINATION

> See also subdivision ARTIFICIAL INSEMINATION under particular animals, e.g., CATTLE—ARTIFICIAL INSEMINATION

ARTIFICIAL INTELLIGENCE

ARTILLERY

ARTISTS

> See also names of specific artists

ARTS

ASBESTOS DUST

ASCETICISM

ASIAN AMERICANS

ASIAN STUDENTS

ASPHALT

ASPHALT ROCK

ASSASSINATION

> See also subdivision ASSASSINATION under names of specific persons

ASSAULT AND BATTERY

ASSAYING

ASSEMBLY, RIGHT OF

ASSERTIVENESS TRAINING

ASSESSMENT

Astrodynamics

> See

> ASTRONAUTICS

ASTROLOGY

ASTRONAUTICS

> See also

> SPACE FLIGHT

ASTRONAUTS

ASTRONOMY

ASTROPHYSICS

ASYLUM, RIGHT OF

ASYLUMS

ATHEISM

ATHLETICS

ATLASES

ATMOSPHERE

ATOMIC BOMB

Atomic bomb shelters

> See

> NUCLEAR BOMB SHELTERS

Atomic bomb testing

> See NUCLEAR WEAPONS TESTING

Atomic bomb victims

> See

> NUCLEAR BOMB VICTIMS

Atomic underground explosions

> See

> UNDERGROUND NUCLEAR EXPLOSIONS

ATROCITIES

ATTICS

ATTORNEYS

ATTORNEYS GENERAL

ATVs

> See

> ALL-TERRAIN VEHICLES

AUCTIONS

> See also specific types, e.g., ART—AUCTIONS

AUDIOVISUAL EDUCATION

AUDIOVISUAL EQUIPMENT

AUDITING

AUDITORIUMS

Auditors

　See

　AUDITING

AUTHORS

Auto mechanics

　See

　AUTOMOBILE MECHANICS

AUTOGRAPHS

AUTOMATED TELLERS

AUTOMATIC DATA COLLECTION SYSTEMS

AUTOMATION

Automobile accidents

　See

　TRAFFIC ACCIDENTS

AUTOMOBILE DRIVERS

AUTOMOBILE DRIVERS TESTS

AUTOMOBILE DRIVING

Automobile driving in winter

　See

　WINTER DRIVING

AUTOMOBILE MECHANICS

AUTOMOBILE PARKING

　See also

　CAMPUS PARKING

　PARKING LOTS

AUTOMOBILE RACING

　See also names of specific races

AUTOMOBILE REPAIR FRAUD

AUTOMOBILE THEFT

AUTOMOBILES

　See also names of specific automobiles, e.g., FORD AUTOMOBILE; CHEVROLET
　　AUTOMOBILE

AUTOMOBILES—ELECTRIC

AUTOMOBILES—SEAT BELTS

AUXILIARY POLICE

AVALANCHES

AVALANCHES—CONTROL

AVIATION

AWARDS

    Subdivision under the name of person and headline/summary

B-1 MILITARY PLANE

B-17 MILITARY PLANE

B-29 MILITARY PLANE

B-47 MILITARY PLANE

Babies

    See

    INFANTS

BABY SITTERS

    See also

    NANNIES

BACKPACKING

BACTERIA

BACTERIAL DISEASES

BACTERIAL DISEASES OF PLANTS

    See also names of specific diseases, e.g., DUTCH ELM DISEASE

BADMINTON (GAME)

Bagpipe and drum music

    See

    BAGPIPE MUSIC

BAGPIPE MUSIC

BAIL BONDSMEN

BAKERY PRODUCTS

    See also names of specific products, e.g., BREAD; COOKIES

BAKING

Baling

> See specific product, e.g., COTTON; WHEAT

BALL GAMES

> See also names of specific games, e.g., BASEBALL

BALLET

BALLET COMPANIES

> See also names of specific ballet companies, e.g., BALLET WEST

Ballistic missile bases

> See

> GUIDED MISSILE BASES

BALLISTIC MISSILES

> See also names of specific missiles, e.g., PATRIOT MISSILE

BALLOON RACING

BALLOONS

BALLOT

> See also

> ELECTIONS

BALLROOM DANCING

BAND MUSIC

BANDS

BANK CREDIT CARDS

BANK FAILURES

BANKRUPTCY

> See also

> BANK FAILURES

BANKS AND BANKING

> See also names of specific banks

Banquets

> See

> DINNERS AND DINING

BAR MITZVAH

BARBERSHOP QUARTETS

BARBERSHOPS

BARBITURATES

BARK BEETLES

BARLEY

BARNS

BAROMETER

BARREL RACING

BARS (DRINKING ESTABLISHMENTS)

BARTENDERS

BASEBALL

    See also specific school names with teams

BASEBALL CARDS

BASEMENTS

Basic training (military education)

    See

    MILITARY EDUCATION—BASIC TRAINING

BASKET MAKING

BASKETBALL

BASQUE AMERICANS

BASS FISHING

BATHS, PUBLIC

BATON TWIRLING

BATS

BEACH EROSION

BEACHES

BEANS

BEARINGS (MACHINERY)

BEAUTY CONTESTS

    See also names of specific contests and persons

BEAUTY SHOPS

BEER

BEES

BEET SUGAR

BELLS

BEVERAGE INDUSTRY

BEVERAGES

Bicycle paths

    See

    CYCLING PATHS

BICYCLES

BICYCLING

BIGAMY

BILINGUALISM

BILLBOARDS

BILLIARDS

BILLS, LEGISLATIVE

BIOLOGY

Biracial children

    See

    CHILDREN OF INTERRACIAL MARRIAGE

BIRTH CONTROL

BIRTH CONTROL CLINICS

BIRTH PARENTS

Birth rate

    See

    VITAL STATISTICS

BIRTHS, MULTIPLE

BISHOPS

    See also subdivision BISHOPS under names of specific denominations, e.g.,
        CATHOLIC CHURCH—BISHOPS

Bison

    See

    BUFFALO

BLACK MUSLIMS

Black soldiers

    See

    SOLDIERS, BLACK

BLACKLISTING

Blacks

    See

    AFRICAN AMERICANS

BLACKSMITHING

BLAST FURNACES

BLASTING

BLIND

BLIZZARDS

BLOOD

BLOOD—PLASMA

BLOOD—TRANSFUSION

BLOOD ALCOHOL

Blue laws

    See

    SUNDAY LEGISLATION

BOATS AND BOATING

BOBSLEDDING

BODYBUILDING

BOILERS

Bomb attacks

    See

    BOMBINGS

BOMBERS

BOMBING AND GUNNERY RANGES

BOMBINGS

BOMBS

BONDAGE (SEXUAL BEHAVIOR)

BONES

BONSAI

BOOK INDUSTRIES AND TRADE

BOOKBINDING

BOOKS

BOOKSELLERS

BOOTS

    See also names of specific types of boots, e.g., COWBOY BOOTS

BORING

    See also

    DRILLING AND BORING

BOSTON MARATHON

BOTANY

BOTTLE INDUSTRY

BOTTLES

BOULDERS

BOUNDARIES

BOUNDARIES, STATE

BOWLING

BOXING

BOY SCOUTS

BOYS

BRAIN

BRAIN DAMAGE

BRAIN DEATH

BRAKES

BRASS ENSEMBLES

BREAD

BREAK DANCING

Breakfast programs, school

    See

    SCHOOL BREAKFAST PROGRAMS

BREAST CANCER

BREAST FEEDING

BREEDING

> See also subdivision BREEDING under names of specific animals, e.g., CATTLE—BREEDING

BREWING INDUSTRY

BRIBERY

BRICK HOUSES

BRICK TRADE

BRIDAL GOWNS

BRIDGE CONSTRUCTION

BRIDGES

Bright children

> See

> GIFTED CHILDREN

Bridle paths

> See

> TRAILS

BROADCAST JOURNALISM

BROADCASTING

BROILING

BROKERS

BRONZE

BRONZES

BROWNIES (GIRL SCOUTS)

BUDDHISTS

BUDGET

BUDGET—UNITED STATES

BUFFALO

BUFFETS

BUILDING AND LOAN ASSOCIATIONS

BUILDING INSPECTORS

BUILDINGS

> See also names of specific buildings, e.g., KENNECOTT BUILDING, or types of buildings, e.g., BARNS; GARAGES; COMMERCIAL BUILDINGS; HISTORIC BUILDINGS

BUILDINGS—EARTHQUAKE EFFECTS

Bulimarexia

> See

> BULIMIA

BULIMIA

BULK SALES

Bull terriers, pit

> See

> PIT BULL TERRIERS

BULLS

BUMPER STICKERS

Bumper strips

> See

> BUMPER STICKERS

BUNGEE JUMPING

BURGLAR ALARMS

BURGLARY

BURIAL

> See also

> CREMATION

BURIAL LAWS

Burial statistics

> See

> VITAL STATISTICS

BURLESQUE (THEATER)

BURN CARE TREATMENT

Burn care units

> See also names of burn care units, e.g., UNIVERSITY OF UTAH BURN CARE UNIT

BURNS AND SCALDS

BUS DRIVERS

BUS LINES

BUSINESS

See also names of specific businesses, e.g., MACY'S

BUSINESS EDUCATION

BUSINESS PARKS

Busing of schoolchildren

See

SCHOOLCHILDREN—TRANSPORTATION

BUTTER

BUTTONS

C-46 MILITARY PLANE

C-47 MILITARY PLANE

C-130 MILITARY PLANE

CABINET WORK

Cabins

See

LOG CABINS

CABLE TELEVISION

CACTUS

Cafeterias

See

RESTAURANTS

CAFFEINE

See also

COFFEE

TEA

CAKE

CAKE DECORATING

CALCULATORS

CALENDARS

CALISTHENICS

CALLIGRAPHY

CALLIOPE

Cambodian Americans

> See

> ASIAN AMERICANS

CAMERAS

CAMOUFLAGE (MILITARY SCIENCE)

CAMPAIGN FUNDS

CAMPERS AND COACHES, TRUCK

CAMPING

CAMPS

CAMPS FOR THE HANDICAPPED

Camps, Military

> See

> MILITARY TRAINING CAMPS

> See also names of specific military camps, e.g., FORT WILLIAMS

Camps, youth

> See

> CAMPS

CAMPUS PARKING

CAMPUS POLICE

CAMPUS-BASED CHILD CARE

CANADIAN AMERICANS

CANALS

> See also names of specific canals

CANCER

CANDLE MAKING

CANDLES

CANDY MAKING

CANNING AND PRESERVING

CANNONS

Canoe trips

> See

> CANOES AND CANOEING

CANOES AND CANOEING

CANVASSING

CANYONS

> See also names of specific canyons, e.g., GRAND CANYON

CAPITAL PUNISHMENT

CAPITOL BUILDING (DENVER)

CAPITOL HILL (SALT LAKE CITY)

CAR POOLS

CARBIDE INDUSTRY

CARBINES

> See also

> RIFLES

CARBOHYDRATES

CARBON

CARD TRICKS

CARDIAC ARREST

CARDIAC MASSAGE

CARDIAC PACEMAKER INDUSTRY

CARDIAC RESUSCITATION

CARDINALS (CATHOLIC CHURCH)

CARDIOLOGY

CARDS

> See also names of specific cards and card games, e.g., BASEBALL CARDS

CARILLONS

CARNIVALS

> See also

> AMUSEMENT PARKS

CARPENTERS

CARPENTRY

CARRIAGE AND WAGON MAKING

Cartographers

    See

    CARTOGRAPHY

CARTOGRAPHY

CARVING (DECORATIVE ARTS)

CASKETS (COFFINS)

CAST IRON

CAST-IRON FRONTS (ARCHITECTURE)

CATECHISMS

CATHEDRALS

    See also names of specific cathedrals, e.g., CATHEDRAL OF THE MADELEINE

CATHODE RAY TUBES

CATHODE RAYS

CATHOLIC CHURCH

CATHOLIC CHURCH—BISHOPS

CATS

CATTLE

CATTLE—ARTIFICIAL INSEMINATION

CATTLE BRANDS

Cattle ranches

    See

    RANCHES

CAVALRY

CAVES

    See also names of specific caves

CELEBRITIES

    See also specific types of celebrities, e.g., ACTORS

Cellars

    See

    BASEMENTS

CEMENT INDUSTRIES

CEMETERIES

> See also names of specific cemeteries

CENSORSHIP

Censorship of the press

> See

> FREEDOM OF THE PRESS

CENSUS

CENTENNIAL CELEBRATIONS

CENTRAL BUSINESS DISTRICTS

CERAMIC INDUSTRIES

CERAMICS

CEREBRAL PALSY

CESAREAN SECTION

CHAIN STORES

Chamber music

> See

> MUSIC

CHAPLAINS

CHARITIES

CHEERLEADING

CHEESE

CHEESE PRODUCTS

CHEMICAL ENGINEERING

CHEMICAL ENGINEERING LABORATORIES

CHEMICAL ENGINEERS

CHEMICAL INDUSTRY

CHEMICAL LABORATORIES

CHEMICAL SPILLS

CHEMICAL WARFARE

CHEMICALS

CHEMISTRY

CHEMOTHERAPY

CHESS

Chiefs of police

    See

    POLICE CHIEFS

CHILD ABUSE

CHILD CARE

CHILD CARE SERVICES

CHILD CARE WORKERS

Child custody

    See

    CUSTODY OF CHILDREN

CHILD MOLESTING

CHILD SUPPORT

CHILD WELFARE

CHILDREN

    See also

    ABUSED CHILDREN

CHILDREN, HOMELESS

CHILDREN IN PORNOGRAPHY

CHILDREN OF ABUSED WIVES

CHILDREN OF ALCOHOLIC PARENTS

CHILDREN OF DIVORCED PARENTS

CHILDREN OF INTERRACIAL MARRIAGE

CHILDREN—EMPLOYMENT

CHILDREN—HOSPITALS

Children's courts

    See

    JUVENILE COURTS

    See also names of specific hospitals

CHINA PAINTERS

CHINESE AMERICANS

CHIROPRACTIC CLINICS

CHIROPRACTORS

CHLORINATION

CHLORINE

CHOCOLATE

CHOCOLATE INDUSTRY

Choirs

>See names of specific choirs, e.g., MORMON TABERNACLE CHOIR

CHRISTMAS

CHURCH AND EDUCATION

CHURCH AND STATE

Church architecture

>See names of specific church buildings

Church bells

>See

>BELLS

CHURCH FINANCE

CHURCH LANDS

CHURCH MEMBERSHIP

CHURCH WORK WITH REFUGEES

Churches

>See names of individual denominations and specific churches

CHURCHES—VANDALISM

CIGARETTE SMOKE

CIGARETTE TAX

CIGARETTES

CINEMATOGRAPHY

CIRCUSES

CISTERCIANS

>See also names of individual abbeys, e.g. CISTERCIAN MONASTERY AT HUNTSVILLE, UTAH

CITIES AND TOWNS—CIVIC IMPROVEMENTS

CITIZENS BAND RADIO

CITIZENSHIP

CITY COUNCILS

CITY PLANNING AND DEVELOPMENT

> See also specific city

CITY TRAFFIC

CITY-COUNTY HEALTH DEPARTMENT

CIVIL DEFENSE

> See also

> AIR DEFENSES, CIVIL

> AIR RAID SHELTERS

> EMERGENCY PREPAREDNESS

CIVIL RIGHTS

CIVIL RIGHTS DEMONSTRATIONS

CIVIL SERVICE

CLAY

CLAY SOILS

CLERGY

CLIFF DWELLINGS

CLIMATOLOGY

CLOCK AND WATCH MAKING

CLOCKS AND WATCHES

CLOG DANCING

CLOSED-CIRCUIT TELEVISION

CLOTHING AND DRESS

CLOTHING FACTORIES

CLOUD SEEDING

CLOWNS

CLUBS

> See also types of clubs and names of specific clubs

COACHING (ATHLETICS)

COAL

COAL GASIFICATION

COAL MINERS

COAL MINES AND MINING

COAL-BURNING POWER PLANTS

Coal-fired power plants

> See

> COAL-BURNING POWER PLANTS

COAL-MINING MACHINERY

Coats of arms

> See

> HERALDRY

COCAINE

COCAINE ADDICTION

COCK FIGHTING

COFFEE

Coffins

> See

> CASKETS (COFFINS)

COINAGE

COINS

> See also

> NUMISMATICS

COKE INDUSTRY

COLD (DISEASE)

COLD STORAGE

> See also

> FARM PRODUCE—STORAGE

COLLECTIBLES

COLLECTION AGENCIES

COLLECTIVE BARGAINING

COLLECTIVE LABOR AGREEMENTS—FIREFIGHTERS

COLLECTIVE LABOR AGREEMENTS—POLICE

COLLEGE ADMINISTRATORS

COLLEGE COSTS

COLLEGE GRADUATES

COLLEGE PRESIDENTS

COLLEGE RADIO STATIONS

COLLEGE SPORTS

 See also subdivision ATHLETICS under names of specific colleges and universities

COLLEGE STUDENTS

COLLEGE TEACHERS

Colleges

 See

 UNIVERSITIES AND COLLEGES

COMMERCE

COMMERCIAL CREDIT FRAUD

COMMUNAL LIVING

COMMUNICATION

COMMUNITY CHURCHES

COMMUNITY COLLEGES

COMMUTERS

COMMUTING

COMPANY TOWNS

COMPOSERS

COMPOST

Compulsory military service

 See

 MILITARY SERVICE, COMPULSORY

COMPUTER CRIMES

COMPUTER DRAWING

COMPUTER ENGINEERING

COMPUTER ENGINEERS

COMPUTER GRAPHICS

COMPUTER NETWORKS

COMPUTER PROGRAMS

COMPUTER-AIDED DESIGN

COMPUTER-ASSISTED INSTRUCTION

COMPUTERS

CONCENTRATION CAMPS

> See also names of specific camps, e.g., TOPAZ INTERNMENT CAMP

CONCERTS

CONCRETE

CONDOMINIUMS

Congressmen

> See LEGISLATORS—UNITED STATES

Congresswomen

> See LEGISLATORS—UNITED STATES

CONIFERS

CONJURING

CONSERVATION AND RESTORATION

> See also subdivision CONSERVATION AND RESTORATION under types of structures and art objects

CONSERVATIONISTS

CONSERVATISM

CONSTABLES

CONSTITUTION OF THE UNITED STATES

CONSTITUTION, STATE

CONSTITUTIONAL CONVENTIONS

CONSTRUCTION INDUSTRY

CONSTRUCTION WORKERS

CONSUMER EDUCATION

CONSUMER PROTECTION

CONSUMERS

CONTACT LENSES

CONTESTS

> See also names of specific contest or type of contest

CONTINUING EDUCATION

CONTRACEPTION

>See also

>BIRTH CONTROL

CONTRACEPTIVE DRUGS

CONTRACEPTIVES

CONTRACTORS

CONTRACTS

Conventions, political

>See

>POLITICAL CONVENTIONS

CONVICT LABOR

Convicts

>See

>PRISONERS

COOKERY

COOKIES

COPPER

COPPER ALLOYS

COPPER MINERS

COPPER MINES AND MINING

COPYING MACHINES

COPYRIGHT

CORNERSTONES

CORONARY HEART DISEASE

CORPORAL PUNISHMENT

CORPORAL PUNISHMENT—SCHOOLS

CORPORATIONS

CORRECTIONAL INSTITUTIONS

CORRUPTION (IN POLITICS)

COSMETICS

COSMOLOGY

COST AND STANDARD OF LIVING

Cottages, summer

>   See

>   VACATION HOMES

COTTON

COTTON MANUFACTURE

COUNCIL OF GOVERNMENTS

Counseling hotlines

>   See

>   HOTLINES (COUNSELING)

COUNSELORS

COUNTERFEITERS AND COUNTERFEITING

COUNTRY LIFE

COUNTY GOVERNMENT

County officers

>   See

>   COUNTY OFFICIALS AND EMPLOYEES

COUNTY OFFICIALS AND EMPLOYEES

COUNTY SCHOOL SYSTEMS

COURT RECORDS

COURTHOUSES

>   See also names of specific buildings

COVENANTS (THEOLOGY)

Coverlets

>   See

>   QUILTS

COWBOY BOOTS

COWBOYS

COYOTES

CRACK (DRUG)

Crafts

    See

    HANDICRAFTS

CREAM

    See also

    MILK

CREDIT

    See also

    BANK CREDIT CARDS

    FARM CREDIT

Credit cards

    See

    BANK CREDIT CARDS

CREDIT UNIONS

CREMATION

    See also

    BURIAL

CRIME AND CRIMINALS

CRIME PREVENTION

Crime syndicates

    See

    GANGS

    ORGANIZED CRIME

CRIMES

    See also names of specific crimes, e.g., BURGLARY; ASSAULT AND BATTERY

Crimes without victims

    See

    VICTIMLESS CRIMES

CRIMINAL BEHAVIOR

CRIMINAL INVESTIGATION

CRIMINAL JUSTICE, ADMINISTRATION OF

CRIMINAL LIABILITY

CRIMINAL PROCEDURE

CRIMINALS

CRISIS INTERVENTION (PSYCHIATRY)

CROP LOSSES

> See also subdivision LOSSES under names of specific crops, e.g., CORN—LOSSES

CROPS

CROSS-COUNTRY SKIING

CRUISE MISSILES

> See also

> BALLISTIC MISSILES

CUB SCOUTS

> See also

> BOY SCOUTS

CULTS

Custodians

> See

> JANITORS

CUSTODY OF CHILDREN

Cycling

> See

> BICYCLING

CYCLING PATHS

CYSTIC FIBROSIS

CZECH AMERICANS

DAIRY CATTLE

DAIRY FARMS

DAIRY INDUSTRY

DAIRY PRODUCTS

> See also names of specific products, e.g., MILK

Dairying

    See

    DAIRY INDUSTRY

DAMS

    See also names of specific dams, e.g., HOOVER DAM

DANCING

DANISH AMERICANS

DATA

Data collection services

    See

    INFORMATION SERVICES

DATA LIBRARIES

Data storage

    See

    INFORMATION RETRIEVAL

DAUGHTERS

DAY CARE CENTERS

    See also

    CHILD CARE SERVICES

    EMPLOYER-SUPPORTED DAY CARE

    NURSERY SCHOOLS

DAYLIGHT SAVINGS TIME

DC-3 (TRANSPORT PLANE)

DEAF

DEAF—HEARING IMPAIRED

DEAFNESS

DEATH AND DYING

Death rate

    See

    VITAL STATISTICS

DEATH THREATS

DEBATES AND DEBATING

DEBTS, PUBLIC

DECONTAMINATION (FROM GASES, CHEMICALS, ETC.)

    See also

    RADIOACTIVE DECONTAMINATION

DEDICATION SERVICES

DEEDS

DEER

Deicing of airplanes

    See

    AIRPLANES—ICE PREVENTION

Delusions

    See

    HALLUCINATIONS AND ILLUSIONS

DEMOCRACY

DEMOGRAPHY

DEMONSTRATIONS

    See also

    CIVIL RIGHTS DEMONSTRATIONS

    RIOTS

Demonstrations of products

    See

    PRODUCT DEMONSTRATIONS

DENTAL CARE

DENTAL CLINICS

DENTAL HEALTH EDUCATION

DENTISTRY

Dentistry clinics

    See

    DENTAL CLINICS

DENTISTS

DEPARTMENT STORES

    See also names of specific stores, e.g., SEARS

Dependents of military personnel

    See

    MILITARY DEPENDENTS

Depression, economic

    See

    DEPRESSIONS

DEPRESSIONS

    May be subdivided by date of depression, e.g., DEPRESSIONS—1929

Desalinization of water

    See

    SALINE WATER CONVERSION

DESERT FAUNA

DESERT FLORA

DESERT GARDENING

DESERTS

    See also names of specific deserts, e.g., ESCALANTE DESERT

Destruction of property

    See

    MALICIOUS MISCHIEF

    VANDALISM

Detention homes, juvenile

    See

    JUVENILE DETENTION HOMES

Development

    See

    PLANNING AND DEVELOPMENT

DIABETES

DIAL-A-MESSAGE TELEPHONE CALLS

DIALYSIS

DIAMONDS

DIAMONDS, INDUSTRIAL

DIARIES

DIESEL MOTORS

DIET

Dieting

    See

    REDUCING DIETS

DIGITAL ELECTRONICS

DIKES

DINNERS AND DINING

DINOSAURS

DIOCESES

Disabled

    See

    HANDICAPPED

DISASTER RELIEF

DISASTER VICTIMS

DISASTERS

    See also specific types of disasters, e.g., AVALANCHES

DISCRIMINATION

DISCRIMINATION BY SEX

DISCRIMINATION IN EDUCATION

DISCRIMINATION IN EMPLOYMENT

DISCRIMINATION IN HOUSING

Discrimination, racial

    See

    RACE DISCRIMINATION

DISEASES

    See also names of specific diseases, e.g., CANCER

DISPLACED HOMEMAKERS

Distance running

    See

    MARATHON RUNNING

Division of powers

   See

   SEPARATION OF POWERS

DIVORCE

DIVORCE SETTLEMENTS

DIVORCED MEN

DIVORCED PEOPLE

DIVORCED WOMEN

DOCKS

DOGS

Dogs for the deaf

   See

   HEARING EAR DOGS

DOLLHOUSES

DOLLS

DOMESTIC RELATIONS COURTS

DOMESTIC VIOLENCE

DONATION OF ORGANS, TISSUES, ETC.

Donations

   See

   GIFTS

DRAFT REGISTRATION

Draft resistance

   See

   MILITARY SERVICE, COMPULSORY—DRAFT RESISTERS

DRAINAGE

DREDGING

DRESSMAKING

DRILLING AND BORING

   Here are entered works on the drilling and boring of holes in metal, wood, and other
   such materials. Works on the cutting of holes in earth or rocks are entered under
   BORING.

DRINKING AGE

DRINKING AGE—LAWS

DRINKING OF ALCOHOLIC BEVERAGES

DRINKING WATER

DRINKING WATER SANITATION

DRINKING WATER—CONTAMINATION

DRIVER EDUCATION

DROWNING

DROWNING VICTIMS

DRUG ABUSE

    See also specific types of drug abuse, e.g., ALCOHOLISM

DRUG ABUSE—COUNSELING

DRUG ABUSE—PREVENTION

DRUG ABUSE—STUDY AND TEACHING

DRUG ABUSE—SURVEYS

DRUG ABUSE—TREATMENT

Drug pushers

    See

    NARCOTICS DEALERS

Drug stores

    See

    DRUGSTORES

DRUG TESTING

DRUG TRAFFIC

DRUGS

    See also names of specific drugs

DRUGS AND EMPLOYMENT

DRUGSTORES

DRUNK DRIVING

DRUNKENNESS

DRY CLEANING

DRY FARMING

DRY GOODS

DRY ICE

DUDE RANCHES

DUE PROCESS OF LAW

Dunes

    See

    SAND DUNES

DUST

DUTCH AMERICANS

DUTCH ELM DISEASE

DYES AND DYEING

EARLY RETIREMENT

EARTH

Earthquake insurance

    See

    INSURANCE, EARTHQUAKE

EARTHQUAKE ENGINEERING

EARTHQUAKES

Earthquakes and buildings

    See

    BUILDINGS—EARTHQUAKE EFFECTS

EARTHWORKS (ARCHAEOLOGY)

ECHO CANYON

ECLIPSES

ECLIPSES, LUNAR

    May be subdivided by year

ECONOMIC DEVELOPMENT

ECONOMICS

EDUCATION

> See also

> ADULT EDUCATION

> CHURCH AND EDUCATION

EDUCATION AND STATE

EDUCATION, HEALTH

EDUCATION, HIGHER

EDUCATION, PRIMARY

Education, religious

> See

> RELIGIOUS EDUCATION

EDUCATION—FINANCE

Educational discrimination

> See

> DISCRIMINATION IN EDUCATION

EDUCATIONAL EXCHANGES

EDUCATIONAL RADIO STATIONS

EDUCATORS

EGG TRADE

ELECTION FORECASTING

ELECTIONS

> See also subdivision ELECTIONS, and ELECTIONS, [date] under names of individual legislative bodies, e.g., SALT LAKE CITY COUNCIL—ELECTIONS, 1988

Elections, county

> See

> LOCAL ELECTIONS

Elections, municipal

> See

> LOCAL ELECTIONS

Elections, primary

>See

>PRIMARIES

ELECTRIC COMPANIES

>See also names of specific companies, e.g., UTAH POWER AND LIGHT COMPANY

ELECTRIC POWER DISRUPTION

ELECTRIC POWER PLANTS

ELECTROCUTION

ELECTRONIC COMBAT RANGE

ELECTRONIC SURVEILLANCE

ELEMENTARY SCHOOLS

Elevators, grain

>See

>GRAIN ELEVATORS

EMERGENCY

EMERGENCY COMMUNICATION SYSTEMS

EMERGENCY FOOD SUPPLY

EMERGENCY HOUSING

EMERGENCY MEDICAL PERSONNEL

>See also

>EMERGENCY MEDICAL TECHNICIANS

>PARAMEDICS

EMERGENCY MEDICAL SERVICES

>See also HOSPITALS—EMERGENCY SERVICES, PARAMEDICS, EMERGENCY MEDICAL PERSONNEL as well as subdivisions AMBULANCE SERVICE and HOSPITALS under names of cities, e.g., DALLAS—AMBULANCE SERVICE and SEATTLE—HOSPITALS

EMERGENCY MEDICAL TECHNICIANS

>See also

>EMERGENCY MEDICAL PERSONNEL

>PARAMEDICS

EMERGENCY POWER SUPPLY

EMERGENCY PREPAREDNESS

EMERGENCY ROAD SERVICE

EMERGENCY TRANSPORTATION

EMERGENCY VEHICLES

EMIGRATION AND IMMIGRATION

EMIGRATION AND IMMIGRATION LAW

EMISSIONS TESTING

EMPLOYEES, RELOCATION OF

EMPLOYER-SUPPORTED DAY CARE

Employment discrimination

    See

    DISCRIMINATION IN EMPLOYMENT

ENDANGERED SPECIES

Energy assistance for the poor

    See

    POOR—ENERGY ASSISTANCE

ENERGY CONSERVATION

ENGINEERING

ENGINEERS

ENTERTAINERS

ENTERTAINING

Enthusiasts (fans)

    See

    FANS (PERSONS)

ENTREPRENEURS

ENVIRONMENTAL ENGINEERING

ENVIRONMENTAL HEALTH

ENVIRONMENTAL IMPACT STATEMENTS

ENVIRONMENTAL LAW

ENVIRONMENTAL MONITORING

ENVIRONMENTAL POLICY

ENVIRONMENTAL PROTECTION

ENVIRONMENTAL PROTECTION AGENCY

ENVIRONMENTAL TESTING

ENVIRONMENTALISTS

EPIDEMICS

>See also names of communicable diseases, e.g., CHOLERA; YELLOW FEVER

Equal opportunity employment

>See

>AFFIRMATIVE ACTION PROGRAMS

EQUAL RIGHTS AMENDMENTS

ERAs

>See

>EQUAL RIGHTS AMENDMENTS

EROSION

>See also

>SOIL CONSERVATION

ESCAPES

EUTHANASIA

EVAPORATION

EVOLUTION

EXCAVATIONS (ARCHAEOLOGY)

EXCHANGE OF PERSONS PROGRAMS

EXECUTIONS AND EXECUTIONERS

EXERCISE

EXHIBITIONISM

EXHIBITIONS

>See also names of specific exhibitions, e.g., RAMSES II

EXHIBITS

Experimentation on animals

>See

>ANIMAL EXPERIMENTATION

EXPLOSIONS

Explosions in mines

    See

    MINE EXPLOSIONS

EXPLOSIVES

EXPLOSIVES, MILITARY

EXTRACURRICULAR ACTIVITIES

EXTRADITION

EYEGLASSES

FABRICS

FACE

FACE—WOUNDS AND INJURIES

FACTORIES

FACTORY AND TRADE WASTE

    See also

    ACID POLLUTION OF RIVERS, LAKES, ETC.

    HAZARDOUS WASTES

FACTORY MANAGEMENT

    See also

    MANAGEMENT

    PERSONNEL MANAGEMENT

Fair housing

    See

    DISCRIMINATION IN HOUSING

FAIRS

Falling stars

    See

    METEORS

FALSE ALARMS

FALSE IMPRISONMENT

FAMILY

    See also

    CHILDREN

    FAMILY REUNIONS

    HEREDITY

    MARRIAGE

    POLYGAMY

Family history

    See

    GENEALOGY

Family planning

    See

    BIRTH CONTROL

FAMILY REUNIONS

FANS (PERSONS)

FARM BUILDINGS

FARM CREDIT

Farm crops

    See

    CROPS

FARM EQUIPMENT

FARM INCOME

    See also

    CROP LOSSES

    AGRICULTURE—ECONOMIC ASPECTS

FARM LAYOUT

FARM LIFE

    See also

    AGRICULTURE

    COUNTRY LIFE

    FARMERS

FARM MANAGEMENT

FARM MANURE

FARM MECHANIZATION

Farm organization

>   See

>   FARM MANAGEMENT

FARM PRODUCE

>   See also

>   CROPS

>   FOOD

FARM PRODUCE—STORAGE

FARM SUPPLIES

FARMERS

FARMS

>   See also

>   DAIRY FARMS

FASCISM

FASCISTS

>   See also

>   FASCISM

FASHION

>   See also

>   CLOTHING AND DRESS

Fashion models

>   See

>   MODELS, FASHION

FASHION SHOWS

FASTS AND FEASTS

>   Here are entered works on religious fasts and feasts.

FATHER AND CHILD

FEDERAL AID

FEDERAL EMPLOYEES

FEDERAL GOVERNMENT

FEDERAL GRANTS

Federal paperwork

    See

    GOVERNMENT PAPERWORK

Federal-state relations

    See

    FEDERAL GOVERNMENT

FENCING

FEMINISM

FIGHTER PLANES

    See also names of specific aircraft, e.g., B-29 MILITARY PLANE

FILLS

Film festivals

    See

    MOVING-PICTURE FESTIVALS

FINANCE

FINANCE, PUBLIC

FIRE

FIRE PROTECTION

Firearms

    See

    WEAPONS

FIREARMS OWNERSHIP

FIREARMS—USE IN CRIME PREVENTION

FIREWORKS

FISHING

FLAGS

FLOATS (PARADES)

FLOOD CONTROL

Flood control dams

    See

    FLOOD DAMS AND RESERVOIRS

FLOOD DAMAGE

FLOOD DAMS AND RESERVOIRS

FLOOD FORECASTING

Flood prevention

    See

    FLOOD CONTROL

Flood protection

    See

    FLOOD CONTROL

FLOODS

FLOWERS

Flying bombs

    See

    GUIDED MISSILES

Flying saucers

    See

    UFOs

FOG

FOG—CONTROL

FOOD

Food aid programs

    See

    FOOD RELIEF

Food assistance programs

    See

    FOOD RELIEF

FOOD CONTAMINATION

FOOD PRICES

FOOD RELIEF

FOOD SUPPLY

FORD AUTOMOBILE

FOOTBALL

FORECASTING

FORECLOSURE

Foreclosure sales

> See

> FORECLOSURE

Foreigners

> See

> ALIENS

Forest planting

> See

> FORESTS AND FORESTRY

FOREST RANGERS

Forest reserves

> See

> NATIONAL FORESTS

Forestation

> See

> FORESTS AND FORESTRY

FORESTS AND FORESTRY

FORGERY

FORGERY—MANUSCRIPTS

FOSSIL

FOSSIL (MAN)

FOSTER GRANDPARENTS

Fraternities

> See

> GREEK LETTER SOCIETIES

FRAUD

Free agency

    See

    FREE WILL AND DETERMINISM

FREE CHOICE OF EMPLOYMENT

FREE PORTS AND ZONES (e.g., CHICAGO FREE PORT)

FREE WILL AND DETERMINISM

Freedom marches

    See

    CIVIL RIGHTS DEMONSTRATIONS

Freedom of assembly

    See

    ASSEMBLY, RIGHT OF

FREEDOM OF INFORMATION

FREEDOM OF SPEECH

FREEDOM OF THE PRESS

FREEMASONRY

FREEMASONS

Freezing

    See

    ICE

FREIGHT AND HANDLING

FRONTIER AND PIONEER LIFE

FRUIT

    See also names of specific fruits, e.g., CHERRIES; APPLES

FUEL

FUEL—LEAKAGE

FUEL—RESEARCH

FUEL—TESTING

FUEL—UNDERGROUND

FUGITIVES FROM JUSTICE

FUR

FUR GARMENTS

FUR TRADE

FUR-BEARING ANIMALS

> See also names of fur-bearing animals, e.g., BEAVERS; MINKS

FURNITURE

Furriers

> See

> FUR TRADE

FUSION RESEARCH

FUTURE LIFE

GAG RULE

GAMBLING

GAME AND GAME BIRDS

> See also names of game animals, e.g., DEER; GROUSE; RABBITS

GAME PRESERVES

Game reserves

> See

> GAME PRESERVES

GAME WARDENS

GAMES

> See also names of specific games, e.g., BASEBALL; BILLIARDS; CHESS

GANGS

GARDENING

GARDENS

GAS

Gas and oil leases

> See

> OIL AND GAS LEASES

GAS INDUSTRY

> Here are entered works on industries based on natural or manufactured gas.

GAS LEAKAGE

GAS, NATURAL

GAS, NATURAL—LAW AND LEGISLATION

GAS, NATURAL—TAXATION

GASES

GASOLINE

GASOLINE—PRICES

Gays

>   See

>   HOMOSEXUALS

GEMS

>   Here are entered works on engraved stones and jewels; works of mineralogical interest are entered under PRECIOUS STONES.

GENEALOGY

GENETICS

GEOGRAPHY

>   Works on the geography of particular places are entered under the name of the place with the subdivision DESCRIPTION AND TRAVEL.

GEOLOGISTS

GEOLOGY

GERM WARFARE

Germs

>   See

>   BACTERIA

GIFTED CHILDREN

GIFTS

GINGERBREAD HOUSES

GIRL SCOUTS

GIRLS

GLACIERS

GLASS

GOATS

GOD

GOD—PROOF

GODS

GOLD

Gold discoveries

    See

    GOLD MINES AND MINING

GOLD MINES AND MINING

GOLF

GOVERNMENT AND THE PRESS

GOVERNMENT BUSINESS ENTERPRISES

GOVERNMENT COMPETITION

GOVERNMENT LIABILITY

GOVERNMENT PAPERWORK

Government responsibility

    See

    GOVERNMENT LIABILITY

GOVERNMENTAL INVESTIGATIONS

    See also names of specific investigative bodies

GRAFT REJECTION

GRAIN

GRAIN ELEVATORS

GRANDPARENT AND CHILD

Gravel industry

    See

    SAND AND GRAVEL INDUSTRY

GRAZING

GRAZING DISTRICTS

GREEK AMERICANS

GREEK LETTER SOCIETIES

    See also names of individual societies, e.g., DELTA KAPPA EPSILON

GROUNDWATER

GROUNDWATER FLOW

GROUP HOMES

    Here are entered works on planned single-dwelling units with unrelated residents.

GROUP PSYCHOTHERAPY

GUIDE DOGS

GUIDED BOMBS

GUIDED MISSILE BASES

GUIDED MISSILE INDUSTRIES

GUIDED MISSILE RANGES

GUIDED MISSILE SILOS

GUIDED MISSILES

    See also names of specific missiles, e.g., PATRIOT MISSILE; SILKWORM

GUIDED MISSILES—GUIDANCE SYSTEMS

GUIDED MISSILES—TESTING

GUMS AND RESINS

Gun ownership

    See

    FIREARMS OWNERSHIP

GUNNERY

Gunnery ranges

    See

    BOMBING AND GUNNERY RANGES

GUNPOWDER

Guns

    See

    WEAPONS

GYMNASTICS

GYROSCOPES

HABITAT (ECOLOGY)

HAIR

Half-breed Indians

See

NATIVE AMERICANS—MIXED BLOOD

HALFWAY HOUSES

HALLUCINATIONS AND ILLUSIONS

HALLUCINOGENIC DRUGS

See also

DRUG ABUSE

HANDICAPPED

HANDICRAFTS

HAND-TO-HAND COMBAT

HANG GLIDING

HANUKKAH

HARDWOODS

HARNESS

HARNESS RACING

Hazardous waste disposal

See

HAZARDOUS WASTES

HAZARDOUS WASTE TREATMENT FACILITIES

HAZARDOUS WASTES

HAZARDOUS WASTES—INCINERATION

HAZARDOUS WASTES—TRANSPORTATION

HEAD START PROGRAMS

HEALTH ATTITUDES

HEALTH EDUCATION

HEALTH FACILITIES

Health insurance

See

INSURANCE, HEALTH

HEALTH MAINTENANCE ORGANIZATIONS

Health services

    See

    MEDICAL CARE

Health spas

    See

    PHYSICAL FITNESS CENTERS

HEARING

HEARING AIDS

Hearing defects

    See

    HEARING DISORDERS

HEARING DISORDERS

HEARING EAR DOGS

HEARING IMPAIRED

    See also

    DEAF

HEARSES (VEHICLES)

HEART

HEART, ARTIFICIAL

HEART, MECHANICAL

Heart-lung machine

    See

    HEART, MECHANICAL

HEAT

HEATING

HELICOPTERS

HERALDRY

HEREDITY

HEX SIGNS

HIDES AND SKINS

> See also
>
> FUR
>
> LEATHER

High jumping

> See
>
> JUMPING

HIGH SCHOOL GRADUATES

> Works on graduates in relation to their alma mater are entered under [NAME OF SCHOOL]—ALUMNI.

HIGH SCHOOLS

> See also names of specific high school, e.g., PROVO HIGH SCHOOL

HIGH-FIBER DIET

HIGH-FIDELITY SOUND SYSTEMS

HIGH-SPEED AERONAUTICS

> See also
>
> AIRPLANES—JET PROPULSION

HIGHWAY DEPARTMENTS

HIGHWAY ENGINEERING

> See also
>
> ROADS

Highway patrols

> See
>
> TRAFFIC POLICE

Hijacking of aircraft

> See
>
> AIRLINES—HIJACKING

HIKING

HISPANIC AMERICANS

> Here are entered works on U.S. citizens of Latin American descent.

HISTORIC BUILDINGS

> See also names of specific buildings

HISTORIC DISTRICTS

>See also names of specific districts

HIT-AND-RUN DRIVERS

HMOs

>See

>HEALTH MAINTENANCE ORGANIZATIONS

HOLDING COMPANIES

HOLIDAYS

>See also names of specific holidays, e.g., CHRISTMAS

HOME ACCIDENTS

HOME ACCIDENTS—PREVENTION

HOME AND SCHOOL

HOME BUSINESS

Home buying

>See

>HOUSE BUYING

HOME CARE SERVICES

HOME ECONOMICS

HOME OWNERSHIP

HOME SCHOOLING

HOMELESS CHILDREN

HOMELESS PERSONS

HOMELESSNESS

Homemakers, men

>See

>HOUSE HUSBANDS

HOMICIDE

>See also

>MURDER

HOMICIDE INVESTIGATION

HOMOSEXUALS

HONEY

HORMONES

HORSE BREEDERS

HORSE RACING

HORSE SHOWS

HORSE STEALING

HORSE TRADING

HORSEMANSHIP

HORSES

HORTICULTURE

HOSPITAL AND COMMUNITY

HOSPITAL CARE

HOSPITAL UTILIZATION

HOSPITALS

>See also names of specific hospitals, e.g., HOLY CROSS HOSPITAL

HOSPITALS—EMERGENCY SERVICES

HOSTAGES

HOT-AIR BALLOONS

Hotel detectives

>See

>HOUSE DETECTIVES

HOTELS, TAVERNS, ETC.

HOTLINES (COUNSELING)

>See also

>CRISIS INTERVENTION (PSYCHIATRY)

Hours of labor

>See

>WORK SCHEDULES

HOUSE BUYING

HOUSE DETECTIVES

HOUSE HUSBANDS

House trailers

> See

> MOBILE HOMES

HOUSEPLANTS

HOUSING

Housing, discrimination in

> See

> DISCRIMINATION IN HOUSING

HOUSING POLICY

HOUSING SUBSIDIES

HUMAN BIOLOGY

HUMAN ECOLOGY

HUMIDITY

HUMILITY

Humor

> See

> WIT AND HUMOR

HUNTERS

HUNTING

HUNTING DOGS

HUNTING GUNS

> See also

> CARBINES

> RIFLES

HUSBAND AND WIFE

HYDRAULIC ENGINEERING

HYDRAULIC STRUCTURES

HYDROELECTRIC POWER PLANTS

HYGIENE

> Here are entered works on personal body care and cleanliness.

HYMNS

HYPERACTIVE CHILDREN

HYPNOTISM

ICE

    See also

    DRY ICE

Ice control (roads)

    See

    ROADS—SNOW AND ICE CONTROL

ICE CREAM

ICE CRYSTALS

ICE FISHING

ICE PREVENTION

Illegal aliens

    See

    ALIENS, ILLEGAL

Illegal strikes

    See

    WILDCAT STRIKES

ILLEGITIMACY

ILLITERACY

Illusions

    See

    HALLUCINATIONS AND ILLUSIONS

ILLUSTRATORS

IMAGING SYSTEMS

IMMUNITY

    Here are entered works on preventive medicine.

IMMUNIZATION

IMPEACHMENTS

IMPLANTS, ARTIFICIAL

IMPOSTORS

IMPRISONMENT

Incarceration

> See
>
> IMPRISONMENT

INCINERATION

INCINERATORS

INCOME

INCOME TAX

Indecent exposure

> See
>
> EXHIBITIONISM

Indian crafts

> See NATIVE AMERICAN CRAFTS

Indians

> See NATIVE AMERICANS

INDUSTRIAL ACCIDENTS

INDUSTRIAL DEVELOPMENT BONDS

INDUSTRIAL ORGANIZATION

INDUSTRIAL SAFETY

Industrial uses of space

> See
>
> SPACE INDUSTRIALIZATION

INDUSTRIALIZATION

INDUSTRY

Industry in space

> See
>
> SPACE INDUSTRIALIZATION

INFANT HEALTH SERVICES

INFANTRY

INFANTS

INFECTION

INFLAMMABLE LIQUIDS

INFLATION (FINANCE)

Information, freedom of

   See

   FREEDOM OF INFORMATION

INFORMATION NETWORKS

INFORMATION RETRIEVAL

INFORMATION SERVICES

Information storage

   See

   INFORMATION RETRIEVAL

INSCRIPTIONS

INSECTICIDES

INSECTS

INSECTS—CONTROL

INSTALLMENT PLAN

INSTINCT

INSTRUMENT FLYING

INSULATION (HEAT)

INSURANCE

INSURANCE COMPANIES

INSURANCE, EARTHQUAKE

INSURANCE, HEALTH

INTEGRATED CIRCUITS

INTELLIGENCE TESTS

INTENSIVE CARE UNITS

INTERIOR DESIGN

Intermarriage

   See

   INTERRACIAL MARRIAGE

   MARRIAGE, MIXED

INTERNAL COMBUSTION ENGINES

INTERNATIONAL RELATIONS

INTERNATIONAL RELIEF

INTERNATIONAL ORDER OF JOB'S DAUGHTERS

Internment camps

> See

> CONCENTRATION CAMPS

INTERRACIAL ADOPTION

INTERRACIAL MARRIAGE

> See also

> CHILDREN OF INTERRACIAL MARRIAGE

INTERVIEWS

> Interviews of specific persons are entered under the name of the person.

INVENTIONS

INVENTORS

Investigations

> See

> CRIMINAL INVESTIGATIONS

> GOVERNMENTAL INVESTIGATIONS

INVESTMENT OF PUBLIC FUNDS

INVESTMENT TRUSTS

INVESTMENTS

IRON

IRON AND STEEL WORKERS

IRON FOUNDING

IRRIGATION

IRRIGATION CANALS

IRRIGATION DISTRICTS

IRRIGATION FARMING

IRRIGATION WATER

JANITORS

JAPANESE

JAZZ FESTIVALS

JET PLANES

JET PLANES—NOISE

JET PROPULSION

JEWELRY

JIU-JITSU

JOB EVALUATION

Job safety

    See

    INDUSTRIAL SAFETY

JOB SATISFACTION

JOB STRESS

Job training

    See

    OCCUPATIONAL TRAINING

Jobless people

    See

    UNEMPLOYED

Joblessness

    See

    UNEMPLOYMENT

JOINTS (ENGINEERING)

Jokes

    See

    WIT AND HUMOR

JOURNALISM

JOURNALISTS

Journeys

    See

    VOYAGES AND TRAVELS

JUDAISM

JUDGES

JUDGMENTS

JUDICIAL ERROR

JUDICIAL REVIEW

JUDICIAL SYSTEM

JUDO

JUMPING

JUNIOR COLLEGES

JUNK MAIL

JURISDICTION

Justice, miscarriage of

    See

    JUDICIAL ERROR

JUSTICES OF THE PEACE

JUVENILE COURTS

JUVENILE DELINQUENCY

JUVENILE DETENTION CENTER

JUVENILE DETENTION HOMES

KIDNAPPING

    See also

    ABDUCTION

Kidney, artificial

    See

    ARTIFICIAL KIDNEY

KINDERGARTEN

    See also

    EDUCATION

    NURSERY SCHOOLS

    PRESCHOOL

KNITTING

LABELS

LABOR AND LABORING CLASSES

>　See also
>
>　ALIEN LABOR
>
>　CHILDREN—EMPLOYMENT
>
>　MIGRANT LABOR
>
>　MIGRANT LABORERS
>
>　OCCUPATIONAL TRAINING
>
>　OCCUPATIONS
>
>　PART-TIME EMPLOYMENT
>
>　PROFESSIONS
>
>　STRIKES AND LOCKOUTS
>
>　UNEMPLOYED
>
>　WAGES
>
>　WOMEN—EMPLOYMENT

Labor arbitration

>　See also
>
>　ARBITRATION, INDUSTRIAL

LABOR DISPUTES

>　See also
>
>　STRIKES AND LOCKOUTS

Labor negotiations

>　See
>
>　ARBITRATION, INDUSTRIAL

LABORATORY ANIMALS

>　See also headings for specific animals, e.g., DOGS AS LABORATORY ANIMALS; HAMSTERS AS LABORATORY ANIMALS

LAKES

>　See also names of specific lakes, e.g., LAKE SUPERIOR; BUCK'S LAKE

Land

>　See
>
>　LAND USE

LAND SALES

Land slides

> See

> LANDSLIDES

LAND SUBDIVISION

LAND USE

> See also

> AGRICULTURE

> REAL ESTATE BUSINESS

> ZONING

Landfills

> See

> FILLS

LANDLORD AND TENANT

LANDSLIDES

LAW

> See also

> LAWYER

> LEGISLATION

> STATUTE

LAW ENFORCEMENT

Lawsuits

> See

> ACTIONS AND DEFENSES

LAWYER

LEATHER

LEGISLATION

Legislative bills

> See

> BILLS, LEGISLATIVE

LEGISLATIVE BODIES

> See also names of individual legislative bodies, e.g., OHIO HOUSE

LEGISLATORS

LEGISLATORS—UNITED STATES

LEUKEMIA, RADIATION-INDUCED

LIBERALISM

LIBERTARIANISM

LIBRARIES

    See also names of specific libraries, e.g., CLAY COUNTY LIBRARY

LIBRARIES AND THE DEAF

LIBRARY SCIENCE

LIFE IMPRISONMENT

LIQUOR LAWS

LITTERING

LIVESTOCK

LOBBYISTS

LOCAL ELECTIONS

LOCAL FINANCE

LOCAL GOVERNMENT

LOCAL LAWS

LOCAL OFFICIALS AND EMPLOYEES

LOCAL TAXATION

LOCAL TRANSIT

LOCAL TRANSIT—FINANCE

LOCAL TRANSIT—PUBLIC OPINION

LOCAL TRANSIT—RATES

LOCAL TRANSIT—RESEARCH

LOCAL TRANSIT—RIDERSHIP

LOG CABINS

LOGGING

LONG-TERM CARE FACILITIES

LOST WORKS OF ART

LOTTERIES

LOVE

Low-income people

    See

    POOR

LUMBER

Lunar eclipses

    See

    ECLIPSES, LUNAR

LYME DISEASE

Male homemakers

    See

    HOUSE HUSBANDS

MALICIOUS MISCHIEF

MALPRACTICE

    See also subdivision MALPRACTICE under names of particular professionals, e.g.,
        PHYSICIANS—MALPRACTICE; NURSES—MALPRACTICE

MAMMALS, FOSSIL

MANAGEMENT

Manslaughter

    See

    HOMICIDE

Man-to-man combat

    See

    HAND-TO-HAND COMBAT

MANUFACTURERS—DEFECTS

MANURES

MANUSCRIPT DATING

Manuscript depositories

    See

    ARCHIVES

MANUSCRIPTS

Manuscripts—forgeries

    See

    FORGERY—MANUSCRIPTS

MANUSCRIPTS (PAPYRI)

MARATHON RUNNING

    See also names of specific marathons, e.g., BOSTON MARATHON

MARBLE QUARRYING

MARIJUANA

MARINAS

MARINE SAFETY

MARKET SURVEYS

MARRIAGE

MARRIAGE COUNSELORS

Marriage, mixed

    See

    INTERRACIAL MARRIAGE

Marriage statistics

    See

    VITAL STATISTICS

MARRIED PEOPLE

MARTIAL ARTS

Masonic orders

    See

    FREEMASONRY

Masonry (secret order)

    See

    FREEMASONRY

MASS MEDIA

MASS MEDIA IN EDUCATION

MASSAGE PARLORS

MATERNAL HEALTH SERVICES

MATERNITY LEAVE

MATHEMATICS

MAYORS

Meals for the elderly

    See

    MEALS ON WHEELS PROGRAMS

MEALS ON WHEELS PROGRAMS

MEASLES VACCINE

MEAT INDUSTRY AND TRADE

MEAT INSPECTION

Meat-packing industry

    See

    PACKING HOUSES

Mechanical heart

    See

    HEART, MECHANICAL

MEDIA SPECIALISTS

MEDICAID

MEDICAID FRAUD

MEDICAL CARE

Medical care of veterans

    See

    VETERANS—MEDICAL CARE

MEDICAL CLINICS

Medical facilities

    See

    HEALTH FACILITIES

MEDICAL RESEARCH

MEDICARE

MEMORIAL DAY

MENTAL HEALTH FACILITIES

MENTAL HEALTH PERSONNEL

MENTAL HEALTH SERVICES

MENTAL ILLNESS

Mental tests

See

INTELLIGENCE TESTS

MENTALLY HANDICAPPED

MENTALLY HANDICAPPED CHILDREN

MENTALLY HANDICAPPED CHILDREN—EDUCATION

MERCHANDISE LICENSING

MERCHANTS

Mercy killing

See

EUTHANASIA

MESCALINE

METEORITES

METEOROLOGICAL SATELLITES

METEOROLOGICAL STATIONS

METEORS

METERS

MEXICAN AMERICANS

MICE

MICROFILM INDUSTRY

MICROFORMS—PRESERVATION AND STORAGE

MIDWIFERY

MIDWIVES

MIGRANT LABOR

MIGRANT LABORERS

Migratory workers

See

MIGRANT LABORERS

MILITARY ACADEMICS

Military air bases

> See

> AIR BASES

MILITARY BASES

> See also names of specific bases, e.g. FORT BRAGG MILITARY BASE

> AIR BASES

> GUIDED MISSILE BASES

> MILITARY POSTS

> NAVY YARDS AND NAVAL STATIONS

MILITARY DEPENDENTS

Military draft registration

> See

> DRAFT REGISTRATION

MILITARY EDUCATION

MILITARY EDUCATION—BASIC TRAINING

Military explosives

> See

> EXPLOSIVES, MILITARY

MILITARY HOUSING

MILITARY MANEUVERS

MILITARY PARKS

Military post exchanges

> See

> POST EXCHANGES

MILITARY POSTS

MILITARY SERVICE, COMPULSORY

MILITARY SERVICE, COMPULSORY—DRAFT RESISTERS

MILITARY SERVICE—DRAFT REGISTRATION

MILITARY SPENDING

MILITARY TRAINING CAMPS

MILK

MILK TRADE

MIMES

MINE ACCIDENTS

    See also names of specific accidents, e.g., WILBURG MINE ACCIDENT

MINE COMMUNICATION SYSTEMS

MINE DRAINAGE

MINE DUSTS

MINE EXAMINATION

MINE EXPLOSIONS

MINE FIRES

MINE INSPECTION

MINE PUMPS

MINE SAFETY

MINE SHAFTS

MINE VENTILATION

MINERAL LANDS

MINERAL LEASES

MINERAL WATER INDUSTRY

MINERAL WATERS

MINERS

    See also specific types of miners, e.g., COAL MINERS; COPPER MINERS

MINES AND MINERAL RESOURCES

MINING CLAIMS

Mining companies

    See

    MINING CORPORATIONS

MINING CORPORATIONS

MINING INDUSTRY AND FINANCE

MINING LEASES

MINING SCHOOL

MINK FARMING

MINORITIES

MINORITIES—EMPLOYMENT

    See also

    AFFIRMATIVE ACTION PROGRAMS

Missile bases

    See

    GUIDED MISSILE BASES

Missile guidance systems

    See

    GUIDED MISSILES—GUIDANCE SYSTEMS

Missile silos

    See

    GUIDED MISSILE SILOS

MISSILE WARHEADS

MISSING CHILDREN

MISSING PERSONS

Missing works of art

    See

    LOST WORKS OF ART

Mixed marriage

    See

    INTERRACIAL MARRIAGE

Mixed-race adoption

    See

    INTERRACIAL ADOPTION

MOBILE HOME PARKS

MOBILE HOMES

Mobile schools

    See

    SCHOOLS, TRAVELING

Model agencies

    See

    MODELING AGENCIES

Model airplanes

    See

    AIRPLANES—MODELS

Model homes

    See

    MODEL HOUSES

MODEL HOUSES

Model railroads

    See

    RAILROADS—MODELS

MODELING AGENCIES

MODELS, FASHION

MODERN DANCE

MONEY

MONUMENTS

MOOT COURTS

MOPEDS

MORTGAGE BANKS

MORTGAGE BONDS

Mortgage companies

    See

    MORTGAGE BANKS

Mortgage foreclosure

    See

    FORECLOSURE

MORTUARY CHAPELS

MOSQUITO CONTROL

MOTELS

MOTHERS

Mothers, working

    See

    WORKING MOTHERS

Motion picture festivals

　　See

　　MOVING-PICTURE FESTIVALS

Motion pictures

　　See

　　MOVING PICTURES

MOTOR BUS LINES

MOTOR VEHICLES

MOTOR VEHICLES—POLLUTION CONTROL DEVICES

MOTORBOATS

Mountain climbers

　　See

　　MOUNTAINEERS

Mountain climbing

　　See

　　MOUNTAINEERING

MOUNTAINEERING

MOUNTAINEERING ACCIDENTS

MOUNTAINEERS

MOUNTAINS—UTAH

Movies

　　See

　　MOVING PICTURES

MOVING PICTURES

MOVING PICTURES AND CHILDREN

MOVING PICTURES—AWARDS

MOVING PICTURES—CENSORSHIP

MOVING-PICTURE FESTIVALS

MOVING-PICTURE INDUSTRY

MOVING-PICTURE THEATERS

MUDFLOWS

MUNICIPAL BUDGETS

MUNICIPAL BUILDINGS

Municipal elections

>   See

>   LOCAL ELECTIONS

MUNICIPAL GOVERNMENT

MUNICIPAL OFFICIALS AND EMPLOYEES

Municipal taxation

>   See

>   LOCAL TAXATION

MUNICIPAL WATER SUPPLY

MURDER

>   See also

>   HOMICIDE

MUSEUMS

>   See also names of specific museums

MUSIC

MUSIC FESTIVALS

MUSICIANS

>   See also types of musicians, e.g., FLUTE PLAYERS; PIANISTS; SINGERS

Mutual funds

>   See

>   INVESTMENT TRUSTS

MX MISSILE

NANNIES

NARCOTICS DEALERS

NATIONAL FORESTS

NATIONAL LIBRARY WEEK

NATIONAL PARKS AND RESERVES

    See also

    FOREST RESERVES

    MONUMENTS

    WILDERNESS AREAS

NATIONAL PARKS AND RESERVES—INTERPRETIVE PROGRAMS

NATIVE AMERICAN CRAFTS

NATIVE AMERICANS

    See also names of specific tribes, e.g., NAVAJO; UTE, etc.

NATIVE AMERICANS—ANTIQUITIES

NATIVE AMERICANS—DWELLINGS

NATIVE AMERICANS—ECONOMIC CONDITIONS

NATIVE AMERICANS—EDUCATION

NATIVE AMERICANS—GOVERNMENT RELATIONS

NATIVE AMERICANS—MIXED BLOOD

NATIVE AMERICANS—SOCIAL LIFE AND CUSTOMS

NATIVE AMERICANS—TREATIES

NATIVE AMERICANS—WAR

NATURAL BRIDGES

NATURAL DISASTER WARNING SYSTEMS

Natural gas

    See

    GAS, NATURAL

NATURE TRAILS

Navaho

    See

    NAVAJO

NAVAJO

Navajo sand paintings

    See

    SAND PAINTINGS

NAVAL RESERVES

NAVY YARDS AND NAVAL STATIONS

NEIGHBORHOOD GOVERNMENT

NEIGHBORHOOD IMPROVEMENT PROGRAMS

NEW YORK CITY MARATHON

NEWS PHOTOGRAPHERS

NEWSPAPERS

    See also

    PERIODICALS

NIGHTCLUBS

NOISE CONTROL

Noise prevention

    See

    NOISE CONTROL

Nordic skiing

    See

    CROSS-COUNTRY SKIING

NOTARIES

Notary public

    See

    NOTARIES

NUCLEAR ARMS CONTROL

NUCLEAR BOMB

NUCLEAR BOMB—VICTIMS

NUCLEAR DISARMAMENT

NUCLEAR POWER PLANTS

Nuclear waste disposal

    See

    RADIOACTIVE WASTE DISPOSAL

Nuclear wastes

    See

    RADIOACTIVE WASTES

NUCLEAR WEAPONS

NUCLEAR WEAPONS TESTING

NUMISMATICS

NUNS

Nurse midwives

    See

    MIDWIVES

NURSE PRACTITIONERS

NURSERIES (HORTICULTURE)

NURSERY SCHOOLS

    See also

    DAY CARE CENTERS

    EDUCATION

    KINDERGARTEN

    PRESCHOOL

NURSES

NURSING

NURSING HOMES

NUTRITION

OBITUARIES

OBSCENITY

Occupational stress

    See

    JOB STRESS

OCCUPATIONAL TRAINING

OCCUPATIONS

ODOR CONTROL

Odor—control

    See

    ODOR CONTROL

OFFICE BUILDINGS

OIL AND GAS LEASES

OIL INDUSTRIES

OIL INDUSTRY WORKERS

OIL POLLUTION OF WATER

Oil refineries

    See

    PETROLEUM REFINERIES

OIL SANDS

OIL SHALE INDUSTRY

    See also

    SHALE OILS

OLYMPIC GAMES

OPERA

OPERATION DESERT SHIELD

OPTICAL ILLUSIONS

ORDINANCES, MUNICIPAL

ORGANIZED CRIME

Organs—transplantation

    See

    TRANSPLANTATION OF ORGANS

OUTDOOR RECREATION

OUTLAWS

OUT-OF-STATE STUDENTS

Out-of-work people

    See

    UNEMPLOYED

Ownership of firearms

    See

    FIREARMS OWNERSHIP

PACIFIC RAILROADS

PACIFIC WAGON ROADS

PACKHORSE CAMPING

PACKING HOUSES

PAGEANTS

PAINT INDUSTRY AND TRADE

PAINTING

PALEONTOLOGY

PAMPHLETS

Panic (economic)

> See

> DEPRESSIONS

PAPYRI, EGYPTIAN

> See also

> MANUSCRIPTS (PAPYRI)

Papyrus manuscripts

> See

> MANUSCRIPTS (PAPYRI)

PARACHUTING

PARADE

> See also

> FLOATS (PARADES)

PARAMEDICS

> See also

> EMERGENCY MEDICAL PERSONNEL

> EMERGENCY MEDICAL TECHNICIANS

PARENT AND CHILD

> See also

> CHILD ABUSE

> CHILDREN OF ALCOHOLIC PARENTS

> CHILDREN OF DIVORCED PARENTS

> PARENTING

> SINGLE-PARENT FAMILY

PARENTHOOD

PARENTING

> Here are entered works on skills, attributes, and attitudes needed for parenthood.

PARENTS

> See also

> BIRTH PARENTS

PARENT-TEACHER RELATIONSHIP

PARK RANGERS

> See also

> FOREST RANGERS

Parking, automobile

> See

> AUTOMOBILE PARKING

PARKING LOTS

PARKING METERS

PARKS—UTAH

> See also names of specific parks, e.g., GRAND TETON NATIONAL PARK (WYOMING)

PARTNERSHIP

PART-TIME EMPLOYMENT

PASSIVE SMOKING

PATENTS

> See also [ITEM NAME]—patents

Paths

> See

> TRAILS

Patients

> See subdivision PATIENTS under individual diseases and parts of the body

PEACH

PEACH INDUSTRY

Pediatric hospitals

> See

> CHILDREN—HOSPITALS

PEDIATRICIANS

PEDIATRICS

Pedigrees

>See

>GENEALOGY

>HERALDRY

PEDODONTICS

>See also

>DENTISTRY

PENSIONS

People, divorced

>See

>DIVORCED PEOPLE

People, married

>See

>MARRIED PEOPLE

People, single

>See

>SINGLE PEOPLE

People, unmarried

>See

>SINGLE PEOPLE

PERFORMING ARTS

PERIODICALS

PERSIAN GULF CRISIS

PERSIAN GULF WAR—PROTESTERS

Personal income

>Soo

>INCOME

PERSONNEL MANAGEMENT

PESTICIDES

PETITIONS

Petroglyphs

    See

    PICTURE WRITING

    ROCK PAINTINGS

PETROLEUM

PETROLEUM CHEMICALS

PETROLEUM CONSERVATION

PETROLEUM ENGINEERING

PETROLEUM PRODUCTS

PETROLEUM REFINERIES

PETROLEUM WASTE

PETROLEUM WORKERS

PETROLEUM—STORAGE

PEYOTE

PEYOTISM

Pharmacies

    See

    DRUGSTORES

PHARMACISTS

PHARMACY COLLEGES

PHEASANT HUNTING

PHEASANTS

PHILANTHROPISTS

PHILOSOPHY AND RELIGION

PHOTOGRAPHERS

PHOTOGRAPHIC INTERPRETATION

PHOTOGRAPHIC SURVEYING

PHOTOGRAPHY

PHYSICAL EDUCATION AND TRAINING

    See also

    ATHLETICS

    COLLEGE SPORTS

PHYSICAL FITNESS

PHYSICAL FITNESS CENTERS

PHYSICAL THERAPISTS

PHYSICAL THERAPY

PHYSICALLY HANDICAPPED

    See also

    BLIND

    DEAF

    PHYSICALLY HANDICAPPED CHILDREN

    SOCIAL WORK WITH THE PHYSICALLY HANDICAPPED

PHYSICALLY HANDICAPPED CHILDREN

PHYSICIANS

PHYSICS

PHYSIOLOGY

PIANISTS

PICKETING

PICKPOCKETS

Pickup campers

    See

    CAMPERS AND COACHES, TRUCK

PICNIC GROUNDS

Pictographs

    See

    PICTURE WRITING

Picture rocks

    See

    ROCK PAINTINGS

PICTURE WRITING

PICTURE WRITING, INDIAN

Pictured rocks

    See

    ROCK PAINTINGS

Pilotless aircraft

>   See

>   GUIDED MISSILES

PILOTS

PILOTS, MILITARY

PIMPS

PINBALL MACHINES

PINE NUTS

Pinon nuts

>   See

>   PINE NUTS

Pioneer life

>   See

>   FRONTIER AND PIONEER LIFE

PIONEERS

>   See also

>   FRONTIER AND PIONEER LIFE

Pipes, tobacco

>   See

>   TOBACCO—PIPES

PIT BULL TERRIERS

Planned parenthood

>   See

>   BIRTH CONTROL

PLANNING AND DEVELOPMENT

PLANTS

PLANTS—WINTER PROTECTION

PLAYGROUNDS

PLUMBING

POACHING

POETRY

POETS

 See also names of individual poets

POISON CONTROL CENTERS

POISONING, ACCIDENTAL

POISONOUS SNAKES

 See also names of specific snakes or groups of snakes, e.g., KING COBRA; RATTLESNAKES

POLICE

Police, airport

 See

 AIRPORT POLICE

Police, campus

 See

 CAMPUS POLICE

POLICE CHIEFS

POLICE COMMUNICATIONS SYSTEMS

POLICE DOGS

Police officers

 See

 POLICE

POLICE PATROL

POLICE SERVICES FOR JUVENILES

POLICE SHOOTINGS

POLICE SOCIAL WORK

Policemen

 See

 POLICE

Policewomen

 See

 POLICE

POLITICAL ACTION COMMITTEES

POLITICAL CAMPAIGNS

POLITICAL CONTRIBUTIONS

POLITICAL CONVENTIONS

POLITICAL ETHICS

POLITICAL PARTIES

> See also names of specific political parties

Political scandals

> See

> CORRUPTION (IN POLITICS)

POLLUTION

> See also

> AIR POLLUTION

> POLLUTION—CONTROL

> WATER POLLUTION

POLLUTION—CONTROL

POLYGAMY

POOR

POOR—ENERGY ASSISTANCE

POOR—SERVICES FOR

POPULATION

> See also

> BIRTH CONTROL

> CENSUS

PORNOGRAPHY

POST EXCHANGES

POSTAGE STAMP

POSTAL SERVICE

POTASH

POTTERY, ANCIENT

Pottery, prehistoric

> See

> POTTERY, ANCIENT

POTTERY, PRIMITIVE

POULTRY—INSPECTION

Power

> See

> ELECTRIC POWER PLANTS

PRAYER

PRAYER IN THE PUBLIC SCHOOLS

PRAYERS FOR RAIN

PRECIOUS STONES

> See also names of specific precious stones, e.g., DIAMONDS

Predators

> See

> PREDATORY ANIMALS

PREDATORY ANIMALS

> See also names of specific animals, e.g., COYOTES

PREDATORY ANIMALS—CONTROL

PREGNANCY

PREGNANCY, ADOLESCENT

PREGNANT WOMEN

PREMARITAL SEX

Prepaid health plans

> See

> HEALTH MAINTENANCE ORGANIZATIONS

PREPAREDNESS

PRERELEASE PROGRAMS FOR PRISONERS

PRESCHOOL

Presents

> See

> GIFTS

PRESERVATION AND RESTORATION

> See also subdivision CONSERVATION AND RESTORATION under types of structures or art objects

Preservation districts

> See

> HISTORIC DISTRICTS

Preservation of microforms

> See

> MICROFORMS—PRESERVATION AND STORAGE

PRESIDENTIAL CANDIDATES

Presidents, college

> See

> COLLEGE PRESIDENTS

PRESS

Press and religion

> See

> RELIGION AND THE PRESS

Press censorship

> See

> FREEDOM OF THE PRESS

Press photographers

> See

> NEWS PHOTOGRAPHERS

Prevention of crime

> See

> CRIME PREVENTION

Prevention of floods

> See

> FLOOD CONTROL

PRICE WARS

PRIMARIES

Primary education

> See

> EDUCATION, PRIMARY

Primary elections

See

PRIMARIES

PRINTING INDUSTRIES AND TRADE

Prison escapes

See

ESCAPES

Prison labor

See

CONVICT LABOR

PRISONERS

PRISONS

Produce

See

FARM PRODUCE

PRODUCT DEMONSTRATIONS

PROFESSIONS

PRO-LIFE MOVEMENT

PROPELLANTS

See also

ROCKETS (AERONAUTICS)—FUEL

PROPERTY TAX

PROPHECY

PROPHECY (CHRISTIANITY)

PROTESTANT CHURCHES

See also names of Protestant denominations

PROTESTANTS

PRUNING

Psychedelic drugs

See

HALLUCINOGENIC DRUGS

PSYCHIATRIC HOSPITALS

PUBLIC ASSISTANCE PROGRAMS

Public demonstrations

    See

    DEMONSTRATIONS

PUBLIC ENTERPRISES

PUBLIC HEALTH

PUBLIC LAND SALES

PUBLIC LANDS

PUBLIC LIABILITIES

PUBLIC LIBRARIES

PUBLIC OPINION

PUBLIC RECORDS

PUBLIC SCHOOLS

    See also

    HIGH SCHOOLS

    SCHOOLS

PUBLIC UTILITIES

Public welfare

    See

    PUBLIC ASSISTANCE PROGRAMS

PUBLIC WORKS

PUBLIC WORSHIP

PUBLISHERS AND PUBLISHING

PUPPETS AND PUPPET PLAYS

QUALITY OF LIFE

Quality of water

    See

    WATER QUALITY

QUILTING

QUILTS

RABBITS

RABIES

RACE DISCRIMINATION

RACE RELATIONS

RACISM

RADIATION

RADIATION INJURIES

Radiation sickness

    See

    RADIATION INJURIES

RADIATION WARNING SYSTEMS

Radiation-induced leukemia

    See

    LEUKEMIA, RADIATION-INDUCED

RADIO STATIONS

    See also

    COLLEGE RADIO STATIONS

    EDUCATIONAL RADIO STATIONS

RADIOACTIVE DECONTAMINATION

RADIOACTIVE FALLOUT

RADIOACTIVE POLLUTION

RADIOACTIVE WASTE DISPOSAL

RADIOACTIVE WASTES

RADIOACTIVITY

RADIOACTIVITY—PHYSIOLOGICAL EFFECT

RADIOLOGY

RADON

RAFTING

RAILROAD COMPANIES

    See also names of specific railroad companies, e.g., SOUTHERN PACIFIC RAILROAD COMPANY

RAILROAD CONSTRUCTION WORKERS

RAILROAD STRIKE

RAILROAD TERMINALS

RAILROADS

RAILROADS—ACCIDENTS

RAILROADS—CROSSINGS

RAILROADS—MODELS

RAILROADS—RIGHT OF WAY

Railroad—terminals

    See

    RAILROAD TERMINALS

Railway

    See

    RAILROAD COMPANIES

RAIN AND RAINFALL

RANCHES

RANGE MANAGEMENT

RANGE POLICY

RANGELANDS

Rangers, forest

    See

    FOREST RANGERS

Rangers, park

    See

    PARK RANGERS

RANSOM

RAPE

RAPE IN MARRIAGE

Rapids, running of

    See

    CANOES AND CANOEING

RARE BOOK LIBRARIES

RARE BOOKS

READING

REAL ESTATE BUSINESS

REAL ESTATE DEVELOPMENT

Real estate subdivisions

>   See

>   LAND SUBDIVISION

Recorded information telephone calls

>   See

>   DIAL-A-MESSAGE TELEPHONE CALLS

RECREATION

RECYCLING

REDUCING

REDUCING DIETS

Reform schools

>   See

>   REFORMATORIES

REFORMATORIES

REFUGEES

REFUGEES, POLITICAL

REFUSE AND REFUSE DISPOSAL

Registers of birth, etc.

>   See

>   VITAL STATISTICS

REHABILITATION CENTERS

Relief (aid)

>   See

>   INTERNATIONAL RELIEF

RELIGION

RELIGION AND CULTURE

RELIGION AND DRAMA

Religion and education

    See

    CHURCH AND EDUCATION

    RELIGIOUS EDUCATION

RELIGION AND ETHICS

RELIGION AND GEOGRAPHY

RELIGION AND LITERATURE

RELIGION AND SCIENCE

RELIGION AND STATE

RELIGION AND THE PRESS

RELIGION IN THE PUBLIC SCHOOLS

RELIGIOUS EDUCATION

    See also

    RELIGION IN THE PUBLIC SCHOOLS

    SUNDAY SCHOOLS

RELIGIOUS NEWSPAPERS AND PERIODICALS

RELOCATION (HOUSING)

Relocation of employees

    See

    EMPLOYEES, RELOCATION OF

RENT STRIKES

RENTAL HOUSING

RESERVOIRS

    See also names of specific reservoirs, e.g., HARTFORD RESERVOIR; AMES RESERVOIR

Resorts, ski

    See

    SKI RESORTS

RESOURCE PROGRAMS (EDUCATION)

REST HOMES

RESTAURANTS

RETAIL TRADE

RETIREMENT

RETIREMENT COMMUNITIES

REVENUE SHARING

RIDING TRAILS

RIFLES

Right of assembly

> See

> ASSEMBLY, RIGHT OF

Right of asylum

> See

> ASYLUM, RIGHT OF

Right of way (railroads)

> See

> RAILROADS—RIGHT OF WAY

RIGHT OF WAY (TRAFFIC REGULATIONS)

RIGHT TO DIE

Right-to-life movement (anti-abortion movement)

> See

> PRO-LIFE MOVEMENT

RIOTS

RITES AND CEREMONIES

RIVERS

> See also names of specific rivers

Road departments

> See

> HIGHWAY DEPARTMENTS

Road engineering

> See

> HIGHWAY ENGINEERING

ROADS

ROADS—SNOW AND ICE CONTROL

Rock climbers

   See

   MOUNTAINEERS

Rock climbing

   See

   MOUNTAINEERING

Rock drawings

   See

   ROCK PAINTINGS

ROCK PAINTINGS

ROCKET ENGINES

ROCKETRY

ROCKETS

ROCKETS (AERONAUTICS)—FUEL

RODENTS

RODEOS

ROOFING

RUNAWAY YOUTH

RUNNING

Rural life

   See

   COUNTRY LIFE

   FARM LIFE

RURAL MENTAL HEALTH SERVICES

RURAL SCHOOLS

RURAL WOMEN

RURAL YOUTH

SABBATH

SAFETY

SAGEBRUSH

SAILBOATS

SAILING

SALES TAX

SALINE WATER CONVERSION

SALINE WATERS

SALT MINES AND MINING

SALTWATER ENCROACHMENT

Sanctuary (law)

>   See

>   ASYLUM, RIGHT OF

SAND AND GRAVEL INDUSTRY

SAND DUNES

SAND PAINTINGS

SATANISM

Savings and loan associations

>   See

>   BUILDING AND LOAN ASSOCIATIONS

SCANDINAVIAN AMERICANS

SCENIC RIVERS

SCHOOL BOARDS

SCHOOL BREAKFAST PROGRAMS

SCHOOL BUSES

SCHOOL DISTRICTS

SCHOOL FACILITIES

SCHOOL FOOD

SCHOOL LIBRARIES

SCHOOL MANAGEMENT AND ORGANIZATIONS

School playgrounds

>   See

>   PLAYGROUNDS

School prayer

>   See

>   PRAYER IN THE PUBLIC SCHOOLS

SCHOOL SAFETY PATROLS

SCHOOL SUPERINTENDENTS AND PRINCIPALS

SCHOOL VANDALISM

SCHOOL VIOLENCE

SCHOOLCHILDREN—TRANSPORTATION

SCHOOLS

SCHOOLS, TRAVELING

Schools—finance

> See
>
> EDUCATION—FINANCE

Science and religion

> See
>
> RELIGION AND SCIENCE

Scouts and scouting

> See
>
> BOY SCOUTS
>
> GIRL SCOUTS

SCUBA DIVING

SCULPTURE

SEASONAL INDUSTRIES

SEASONAL LABOR

SEAT BELTS

Second-hand smoking

> See
>
> PASSIVE SMOKING

SECRET SOCIETIES

Seeing eye dogs

> See
>
> GUIDE DOGS

SEPARATION OF POWERS

SEWAGE

Sewers

    See

    SEWAGE

SEX COUNSELING

Sex discrimination

    See

    DISCRIMINATION BY SEX

Sex education

    See

    SEX INSTRUCTION

SEX INSTRUCTION

SEX INSTRUCTION FOR CHILDREN

SEX INSTRUCTION FOR YOUTH

SEX OFFENDERS

SEX-ORIENTED BUSINESSES

SHAKEN BABY SYNDROME

    See also

    CHILD ABUSE

SHALE OILS

    See also

    OIL SHALE INDUSTRY

SHEEP

SHERIFF

SHIPS AND SHIPPING

Shooting stars

    See

    METEORS

Shootings by police

    See

    POLICE SHOOTINGS

SHOPPING MALLS

Shore erosion

    See

    BEACH EROSION

SHORT STORIES

SIDEWALKS

SILK INDUSTRY

SILKWORMS

SINGERS

SINGLE PARENTS

SINGLE PEOPLE

SINGLE-PARENT FAMILY

SISTERS (RELIGIOUS)

SKI RACING

SKI RESORTS

SKIERS

Skiing

    See

    SKIS AND SKIING

Skiing accidents

    See

    SKIS AND SKIING—ACCIDENTS AND INJURIES

SKIN DIVING

Skins

    See

    HIDES AND SKINS

SKIS AND SKIING

SKIS AND SKIING—ACCIDENTS AND INJURIES

SKYDIVING

Skyjacking

    See

    AIRLINES—HIJACKING

SKYLAB PROJECT

SLANDER

SMALL BUSINESS

SMOKING

SMUGGLING

SNOW

SNOW FENCES

SNOW REMOVAL

SNOW SCULPTURE

Snow tires, studded

    See

    STUDDED TIRES

SNOWMOBILES

SOCIAL SECURITY

SOCIAL SERVICE

Social work

    See

    SOCIAL SERVICE

SOCIAL WORK ADMINISTRATION

SOCIAL WORK WITH THE PHYSICALLY HANDICAPPED

SOCIAL WORKERS

SOFTBALL

SOIL CONSERVATION

SOILS—LEAD CONTENT

SOILS—TESTING

SOLAR COLLECTORS

SOLAR ENERGY

SOLAR HEATING

SOLAR HOUSES

SOLDIERS

SOLDIERS, BLACK

SONIC BOOM

Sororities

　　See

　　GREEK LETTER SOCIETIES

SPACE FLIGHT

SPACE INDUSTRIALIZATION

SPACE SHUTTLES

　　See also names of specific space shuttle, e.g., COLUMBIA; ENTERPRISE

SPACE STATIONS

SPACE TECHNOLOGY

SPACE VEHICLES—GUIDANCE SYSTEMS

SPACE VEHICLES—PROPULSION SYSTEMS

Spas

　　See

　　PHYSICAL FITNESS CENTERS

Speech, freedom of

　　See

　　FREEDOM OF SPEECH

SPORTS

　　See also names of specific sports, e.g., BASEBALL; TENNIS

SPORTS FACILITIES

Stars, falling

　　See

　　METEORS

STATE BOARDS OF EDUCATION

STATE GOVERNMENTS

STATUTE

Steel workers

　　See

　　IRON AND STEEL WORKERS

Stock ranges

　　See

　　RANGELANDS

STOCKYARDS

STORYTELLING

Straw votes

    See

    ELECTION FORECASTING

Street gangs

    See

    GANGS

STREETS

    See also names of individual streets

STRIKEBREAKERS

STRIKES AND LOCKOUTS

Strikes, illegal

    See

    WILDCAT STRIKES

STUDDED TIRES

STUDENT ACTIVITIES

STUDENT FINANCIAL AID ADMINISTRATION

STUDENT HOUSING

STUDENT LOAN FUNDS

STUDENTS

STUDENTS—FOREIGN

    See also student groups by nationality, e.g., ARAB STUDENTS

SUGAR

SUGAR BEET AS FEED

SUGAR BEET INDUSTRY

SUGAR FACTORIES

SUGAR MACHINERY

SUGAR TRADE

SUGAR WORKERS

SUICIDE

    See also

    YOUTH—SUICIDAL BEHAVIOR

Summer homes

    See

    VACATION HOMES

SUMMER SCHOOLS

SUNDAY LEGISLATION

SUNDAY SCHOOLS

SURGERY, CORONARY

Surgical implants

    See

    IMPLANTS, ARTIFICIAL

SURVIVAL AND EMERGENCY EQUIPMENT

SURVIVAL SKILLS

SWIMMING AND DIVING

TAMPERED PRODUCT

TANNING SALON

Tax assessment

    See

    ASSESSMENT

Tax sharing

    See

    REVENUE SHARING

TAXATION

TAXATION, STATE

TAXIDERMY

TEA

TEACHERS

TEACHERS' UNIONS

TEACHERS—SALARIES, PENSIONS, ETC.

TEENAGE MARRIAGE

Teenage pregnancy

    See

    PREGNANCY, ADOLESCENT

Teenagers

    See

    YOUTH

TELEPHONE

TELEPHONE HARASSMENT

TELEPHONE LINES

TELEPHONE SELLING

TELEPHONE—DIRECTORIES

TELEPHONE—EMERGENCY REPORTING SYSTEMS

Television, cable

    See

    CABLE TELEVISION

TELEVISION PROGRAMS

Terrorist bombings

    See

    BOMBINGS

Testimony

    See

    WITNESSES

TEXTBOOKS

THANKSGIVING DAY

THEATER

THEOLOGY

TOBACCO

TOBACCO—PIPES

TOURIST CAMPS, HOSTELS, ETC.

Toxic wastes

> See

> HAZARDOUS WASTES

TRAFFIC ACCIDENTS

TRAFFIC CONTROL

TRAFFIC LIGHTS

TRAFFIC POLICE

TRAFFIC REGULATIONS

TRAFFIC SAFETY

TRAFFIC SAFETY AND CHILDREN

TRAFFIC SPEED

TRAFFIC VIOLATIONS

TRAILS

TRAMPS

Transient workers

> See

> MIGRANT LABORERS

TRANSPLANTATION OF ORGANS

Transplant rejection

> See

> GRAFT REJECTION

TRANSPORTATION

> See also

> SCHOOLCHILDREN—TRANSPORTATION

TRAPPERS

TRAPPING

TRAPPISTS

> See also

> CISTERCIANS

Truck campers and coaches

> See

> CAMPERS AND COACHES, TRUCK

TRUCK FARMING

TRUCKING

TWINS

UFOs

ULTRALIGHT AIRCRAFT

UNDERGROUND CONSTRUCTION

UNDERGROUND NUCLEAR EXPLOSIONS

Underground nuclear testing

> See

> UNDERGROUND NUCLEAR EXPLOSIONS

UNDERGROUND STORAGE

Underground telephone lines

> See

> TELEPHONE LINES

Underground utility lines

> See

> UTILITY LINES

UNDERTAKERS

Underwater swimming

> See

> SKIN DIVING

Undocumented aliens

> See

> ALIENS, ILLEGAL

UNEMPLOYED

> See also

> MIGRANT LABORERS

UNEMPLOYMENT

UNFAIR LABOR PRACTICES

Unidentified flying objects

    See

    UFOs

Uninsured motorist insurance

    See

    INSURANCE

UNION PACIFIC RAILROAD

UNITED STATES

UNITED STATES. AIR FORCE

UNITED STATES. ARMY

UNITED STATES. ARMY AIR FORCES

UNITED STATES. ARMY. AIR CORPS

UNITED STATES. CONGRESS

UNITED STATES. CONGRESS. HOUSE

UNITED STATES. CONGRESS. SENATE

UNITED STATES. DEPARTMENT OF LABOR

UNITED STATES. INTERNAL REVENUE SERVICE

UNITED STATES. MARINE CORPS

UNITED STATES. NAVY

UNITED STATES. POLITICS AND GOVERNMENT

    See also

    LEGISLATORS—UNITED STATES

UNITED STATES. SUPREME COURT

UNIVERSITIES AND COLLEGES

UNLAWFUL ENTRY

UNMARRIED COUPLES

UNMARRIED PEOPLE

Upland game birds

    See

    GAME AND GAME BIRDS

URANIUM

URANIUM MILL TAILINGS

Uranium mines

>See

>URANIUM

Urban development

>See

>CITY PLANNING AND DEVELOPMENT

Urban housing

>See

>HOUSING

URBAN RENEWAL

Urban traffic

>See

>CITY TRAFFIC

URBAN TRANSPORTATION

Urban water

>See

>MUNICIPAL WATER SUPPLY

Use of firearms in crime prevention

>See

>FIREARMS—USE IN CRIME PREVENTION

Utilities

>See

>PUBLIC UTILITIES

UTILITY LINES

VACATION HOMES

VACATION SCHOOLS (BAPTIST, METHODIST, ETC.)

VACATIONS

VACCINATION

VACCINES

Vagabonds

> See

> HOMELESS PERSONS

Vagrancy

> See

> HOMELESSNESS

Vagrant children

> See

> HOMELESS CHILDREN

Vagrants

> See

> HOMELESS PERSONS

VALLEYS

VALUE-ADDED TAX

VAMPIRE BATS

VANDALISM

> See also

> SCHOOL VANDALISM

VAULTS

VEGETABLE GARDENING

VEHICLES

> See also names of specific types of vehicles, e.g., AMBULANCES; AUTOMOBILES; BICYCLES; WAGONS

VENDING MACHINES

VENDORS

VENEREAL DISEASE EDUCATION

> See also

> HEALTH EDUCATION

> SEX INSTRUCTION

VENEREAL DISEASES

Venomous snakes

See

POISONOUS SNAKES

VENOMS

VETERANS

VETERANS DAY

VETERANS, DISABLED

VETERANS—MEDICAL CARE

VETERINARIANS

VICE-PRESIDENTIAL CANDIDATES

VICTIMLESS CRIMES

VICTIMS OF TERRORISM

VIDEOTAPE RECORDERS AND RECORDING

VIOLENCE

VITAL STATISTICS

VOCATIONAL EDUCATION

VOCATIONAL GUIDANCE

VOLCANOES

VOLUNTEERS

VOTERS, REGISTRATION OF

See also

VOTING

VOTING

See also

ELECTIONS

VOTING DISTRICTS

VOYAGES AND TRAVELS

WAGES

WALKING

    See also

    HIKING

    TRAILS

WALKING IN SPACE

WARNINGS

Waste, disposal of

    See

    REFUSE AND REFUSE DISPOSAL

WASTE WATER TREATMENT

Watch making

    See

    CLOCK AND WATCH MAKING

WATER

    See also

    DRINKING WATER

    FLOODS

    LAKES

    RAIN AND RAINFALL

    RIVERS

WATER DISTRICTS

WATER METERS

Water, municipal

    See

    MUNICIPAL WATER SUPPLY

Water pollution

    See

    WATER—POLLUTION

WATER QUALITY

WATER RESOURCES DEVELOPMENT

    See also

    FLOOD CONTROL

WATER RIGHTS

WATER—POLLUTION

WATER—STORAGE

WATER—SUPPLY

WEAPONS

Weapons, atomic

    See

    NUCLEAR WEAPONS

WEATHER

Weather satellites

    See

    METEOROLOGICAL SATELLITES

Weather stations

    See

    METEOROLOGICAL STATIONS

Welfare

    See

    CHARITIES

    PUBLIC ASSISTANCE PROGRAMS

WELFARE FRAUD

WELFARE FUNDS

Well boring

    See

    BORING

WHEAT

White-water canoeing

    See

    CANOES AND CANOEING

Wife and husband

    See

    HUSBAND AND WIFE

Wild and scenic rivers

    See

    SCENIC RIVERS

WILDCAT STRIKES

    See also

    STRIKES AND LOCKOUTS

WILDERNESS AREAS

    See also

    NATIONAL PARKS AND RESERVES

WILDERNESS SURVIVAL—PROGRAMS

WILDLIFE CONSERVATION

    See also

    ENDANGERED SPECIES

    NATIONAL PARKS AND RESERVES

    WILDERNESS AREAS

Wildlife management

    See

    WILDLIFE CONSERVATION

WINE AND WINE MAKING

WINTER DRIVING

WINTER SPORTS

    See also names of specific sports

WINTER SPORTS FACILITIES

WINTER STORMS

Winter tires, studded

    See

    STUDDED TIRES

WITNESSES

Woman

    See

    WOMEN

WOMEN

    See also

    FEMINISM

WOMEN—EMPLOYMENT

WOOD-BURNING STOVES

WORK SCHEDULES

WORKING MOTHERS

Yacht basins

    See

    MARINAS

YACHT CLUBS

YACHTS AND YACHTING

    See also

    MARINAS

    SAILING

YODELS AND YODELING

YOM KIPPUR

YOUTH

    See also

    CHILDREN

    RUNAWAY YOUTH

    SEX INSTRUCTION FOR YOUTH

Youth gangs

　　See

　　GANGS

YOUTH—SUICIDAL BEHAVIOR

ZONING

　　See also

　　AIRPORT ZONING

　　ZONING LAW

ZONING LAW

ZOO ANIMALS

ZOOS

Index